PRAISE FOR *THE MOBILE REVOLUT*

C000226065

'The transformation of Orange and T-Mobile into EE had a bit of 'everything, everywhere' about it. Most mergers fail to create value and some collapse into chaos, but the tale of how two struggling British mobile brands propelled the country into the 4G future is one worth telling.' **Nic Fildes, *The Times***

'The EE story was like a business soap opera from start to finish – from the moment that Orange and T-Mobile merged to the drama when BT bought the company. It clearly wasn't plain sailing, but it was ultimately a success – and was fascinating to watch and report on along the way.' **Daniel Thomas, *Financial Times***

'EE was one of biggest brand launches of the past five years. Olaf and Stuart, central characters in its success, narrate the story with aplomb. This is a candid and highly readable account of an ambitious project, offering valuable lessons for marketers, communicators and business leaders alike. The EE campaign exemplifies vision, rigorous focus and adept execution.' **Danny Rogers, Editor in Chief, *PRWeek*, and author of *Campaigns That Shook the World***

'Many books could be written about how the mobile communications industry grew from a cottage industry making car phones for affluent businessmen to the most transformative technology since the invention of the microprocessor. *The 4G Mobile Revolution* is Olaf Swantee's diary of how EE was formed from the merger of Orange and T-Mobile. Swantee has collaborated with another insider, ex-EE Director of Communications and Corporate Affairs Stuart Jackson, to produce a book that will find its natural home in business school classrooms and the Kindles and briefcases of thrusting young Turks eager to find out what management skills are required to make an effective CEO. Swantee gives the reader an enticing peek behind the curtain of the EE story – from clandestine war rooms in a London hotel planning the top-secret merger to establishing the EE brand itself.' **Ian White, Owner and Publisher,** *Mobile News*

The 4G Mobile Revolution

Creation, innovation and transformation at EE

Olaf Swantee with Stuart Jackson

Kogan Page

LONDON PHILADELPHIA NEW DELHI

First published in Great Britain and the United States in 2016 by Kogan Page Limited

2nd Floor, 45 Gee Street
London
EC1V 3RS
United Kingdom

1518 Walnut Street
Suite 900
Philadelphia PA 19102
USA

4737/23 Ansari Road
Daryaganj
New Delhi 110002
India

www.koganpage.com

ISBN   978 0 7494 7939 8
E-ISBN   978 0 7494 7940 4

British Library Cataloguing-in-Publication Data

A CIP record for this book is available from the British Library.

Library of Congress Cataloging-in-Publication Data

Names: Swantee, Olaf, author. | Jackson, Stuart, author.
Title: The 4G mobile revolution : creation, innovation and transformation at
    EE / Olaf Swantee, with Stuart Jackson.
Description: Philadelphia : Kogan Page, 2016. | Includes bibliographical
    references and index.
Identifiers: LCCN 2016020038 | ISBN 9780749479398 (pbk.)
Subjects: LCSH: Creative ability in business. | Leadership. | Long-Term
    Evolution (Telecommunications) | Mobile communication systems–Standards.
Classification: LCC HD53 .S8935 2016 | DDC 338.7/62138456–dc23
LC record available at https://lccn.loc.gov/2016020038

Typeset by SPi Global
Print production managed by Jellyfish
Printed and bound by CPI Group (UK) Ltd, Croydon CR0 4YY

*This book is dedicated to all EE employees
who created a great company*

CONTENTS

About the authors xi
Foreword xiii
Preface xv

01   Inspiration, inventors and innovation 1
Transformative leaders 2
Transformative technologies 5
A transformative telecoms market 8

02   Sleeping with the enemy 15
Genesis of the joint venture 16
Britain's biggest communications company 22

03   A new team to deliver 29
A leadership structure to enable transformation 29
Selecting a team to move the company forward 37
Transforming the management structure 40
Establishing priorities 43
A new leadership style for a new business 44

04   An audacious plan 49
The big bang theory 49
The innovation vs regulation conundrum 51
Building a plan and a vision for the company 58

05   A step change in performance 63
Execution, execution, execution 63
The Performance Management Framework 66
Aligning performance to the vision 67
Setting the direction 68
Instilling clear accountabilities and responsibilities 69
Getting your team to commit 70

The power of the Performance Dashboard 71
The importance of getting to know the
   customer and the front line 72

06   Building a new brand for Britain 75
The secret project 75
Brand transformation 77
Product innovation at the core of your brand 87
A brand-new DNA – from the inside out 96

07   Announcing EE 101
Managing the pressure points 101
The importance of strategic partnerships 107
The communications challenge 110
We are EE 118

08   The challenge of momentum 123
2013 and 2014: the superfast years 123
A technological transformation 126
The ever-evolving network 133
Taking up the challenge of serving half of Britain 136

09   Supercharging sales 147
Breaking records with 4G 147
Transforming a business-to-consumer function 149
Retail transformation 150
Digital transformation 154
Transforming a business-to-business function 158

10   The £12.5 billion business 165
Kick-starting a financial transformation 165
The importance of cash management 167
The key to supplier management 168
Driving revenue profitably 169

11   The culmination of the joint venture 173
A new transformation 173
The integration challenge 175
5G and the video revolution 177
The people of EE 178

Afterword **183**
Endnotes **187**
Index **191**

ABOUT THE AUTHORS

Olaf Swantee

Olaf Swantee led the team that launched EE. He was an Executive Vice President at Orange Group before taking the reins at the UK company formed by the joint venture between Orange and T-Mobile. Prior to joining the telecommunications industry, he worked for IT firms including Hewlett-Packard and Compaq. He is now CEO at Swiss telecoms company Sunrise.

Stuart Jackson

Stuart Jackson led the communications team at EE before running the CEO's office. Prior to this, he was Communications Director at Orange. Before joining the communications industry, Stuart was a journalist; his work appearing in newspapers including the *Daily Telegraph*, the *Daily Mirror* and *The Sun*. He is now Vice President of Communications for Nissan in Europe.

FOREWORD

Technology continues to change our world. It is an unstoppable force that can help drive up education, empower personal independence and deliver global solutions to local problems. And its effect on our world has never been greater than it is today.

It is well documented that the world has changed more in the last 50 years than it ever has before in human history. From the advent of the space race to the home computing revolution, and to the adoption of the mobile phone, we have witnessed a more rapid change in lifestyle and opportunity than ever before.

But in recent years, it is connectivity that has unlocked the true potential of this technological revolution – specifically, the advent of superfast mobile networks that enable people to do more and stay connected, wherever they are.

In many walks of life, countries, companies and communities are accelerating beyond their rivals by using the power of connectivity to circumvent traditional thinking. The M-Pesa revolution in Africa for instance, enabling people to transfer money via text message, has shown how connectivity and currency can align and transform individual and cultural opportunities.

Connectivity provides opportunity and social advancement and opens up the world to those who would previously be isolated and alone.

It's one of the reasons I started the Go ON charity, which recently joined forces with Doteveryone – to show what's possible and support projects that embody how, at scale, technology and connectivity can be a significant driver of social change.

The success of the EE story as a democratizer of high-end technology for the masses was part of that change.

Whether you were born in the 20th or 21st century, whether you live in Silicon Valley or the Rhondda Valley, whether you're at school, in work, at home or retired, technology means we can all be a part of the innovation generation – a generation with connectivity and opportunity at its heart.

Martha Lane Fox
Baroness Lane-Fox of Soho

PREFACE

I'm not good at reminiscing. Looking back at the 'good old days' is a far less appealing option than looking to the future and deciding what we can do next. However, in writing this book I've had to look back and retrace the steps we took in bringing two businesses together to create the number one.

It was a unique plan and an incredible journey. What was achieved by the EE team – from the leadership to the front line, and everyone in between – was nothing short of extraordinary.

I dedicate this book to every single person who helped build the business and supported us in navigating through the good days and the bad. Ultimately, together, we took two businesses worth a combined £8.5 billion, created a new one, and sold it for over £12.5 billion five years later.

This is the story of how we did it, what we got right and where we got it wrong.

I hope it will be useful for someone who is – or aspires to become – a business leader. Although my experience is in the technology industries, I believe that my successes and my mistakes are relevant to many other industries too.

I'm hugely passionate about the industry I work in, but I've found that when I share my experiences – the good, the bad and the ugly – with people who work in other sectors, they have generally found it interesting (until I begin explaining the technical details of how the iPhone 6 chipset improves your signal through voice over Wi-Fi, or how angling a mobile phone antenna in a slightly different position can make a 0.3 per cent improvement in signal quality… that's the passion coming through!)

People who are in business – or want to be in business – will know that the fastest way to learn is to draw on what has been proven to work already. There is no time for a business leader to go through every learning curve from scratch, and doing so would be a painful and dangerous process – both for the individual and the business.

So, throughout this book I've outlined the real examples and techniques that we used in building the EE business in order to illustrate key structures and strategies for leadership.

Mostly, I have tried to blend the two, combining functional business transformation learnings with the EE story itself. If you run a company, are in the middle of your own corporate transformation, or simply want to learn more about business, I hope you'll find it interesting, engaging and, most importantly, useful.

Ours was a superfast experience in every sense of the word, with many moving parts changing and challenging our people and plans at every stage. I have structured this book in a way that keeps the narrative engaging and consumable, with the chapters representing key moments in the short history of building the EE business and brand. While I have attempted to cover the majority of events in a linear timeline, that does mean that some of the topics will have occurred in parallel or in a different order to the way they are represented in this book.

So, the structure of the book allows you to understand the specific transformation of the EE business, but also gives you the possibility to pick and choose certain functional areas that may be specifically relevant to you and the experiences you're going through.

If you're trying to transform the culture of your business, we have a section for that. Perhaps you need to transform your sales organization? There's information on what we did there too, as there is for brand transformation, business-to-business, customer services and so on.

Businesses are in continual phases of transformation. As you progress through the chapters of this book, you may wish to ask yourself how your business is transforming itself and at which point your company is in that transformation.

If you look blankly at that statement and feel it doesn't relate to you, I would question whether your business is performing to its fullest potential. In fact, I would question just how positive the future for your business is. Companies are transforming all the time. If the management of a company stops transforming the organization, processes, people, products, culture and routes to markets, the company is at the beginning of the end.

If people who work for you stop worrying about evolving their ways of working to deliver higher performance, then complacency has crept in – and complacency is the start of a company's decline. It is the start of a company becoming irrelevant.

Often, people will obstruct change. Whatever level you're operating at, if you are a leader trying to drive through change, the following phrases are likely to be familiar to you:

'We tried this in the past – it didn't work.'

'I agree it's important but we simply don't have the resources.'

'I have to focus on the day-to-day business – not three years down the line.'

'I've been with the company for 20 years – I know what works and what doesn't.'

'I can do it, but I don't trust that the other departments can make it happen.'

Most people obstruct change because most people fear change. Maybe they fear it because they're too comfortable. Or perhaps because they're concerned that the new world means they'll have to work in a way they don't like, or aren't used to. Or perhaps they worry that, fundamentally, they won't have a place in the new world. Whatever the reason, you will hear these phrases uttered time and time again during periods of change – both large and small. If you hear them and decide to do nothing, believing that change will be too tough, or destabilizing, then you are in serious trouble. You are the leader of a business in decline.

I once worked for a company called Digital Equipment. I was the chief of staff to the CEO. One of my tasks was to find out why the company's executive board decisions were not executed properly. The decisions were pretty significant, urgent and highly transformative in nature because the company was losing millions of dollars every day (even during weekends). After every board meeting, I wrote an official letter from the CEO and his team to the vice president who was in charge of kick-starting the necessary transformation. It was a waste of time and the content of those letters never resulted in any real action other than yet more discussion among the VPs. The letters were nothing more than a motivation for another meeting to debate the decision. The consensus culture and lack of trust in the leadership of the company inhibited change. It was a great company, but it does not exist anymore.

Another fantastic company that I worked for, Compaq Computer, bought Digital Equipment. Compaq was amazing. The people were great. They were motivating and inspiring, but even they did not manage to truly embrace transformation and become the more services-led and software-centric organization that the business had the potential to become.

The company was ultimately sold to Hewlett-Packard.

HP has missed the smartphone boom. It has missed tablets. It is not leading the 3D printing revolution (for now at least). And it is still a company that – mostly – focuses on hardware only. The business has to transform into software, services and new hardware categories in the future. The good news for HP is that their latest CEO, Meg Whitman, has taken many of the right decisions to get the business back on track.

Overall, the technology industry is very Darwinian. The industrial cycles are typically shorter compared to other markets and increasingly the competitive advantage depends on the ability to attract, to develop, and to retain the best software engineers. Software and services have become the names of the game. Think about the Nokia business story. Apple and Google ate Nokia's lunch, entering – and ultimately dominating – the mobile market because of a superior operating system and set of applications.

The next industry in for a similar revolution is the car industry. I have an app on my phone that allows me to remotely control functions of my electric car – such as managing at what time of the day I will charge the car depending on the cost of electricity. There are less crucial functions (although I really like them) such as turning on the heating in the car while you're still in bed, or honking the horn remotely while the car sits in the parking bay. Now, you might say that honking the horn of a car while you sit in an office is irrelevant and kind of stupid. You are, of course, right. However, it is important to realize that transformation in technology comes increasingly from applications that are consumer-centric and playful.

In the past, most of the technology revolution came from the business-to-business market, with a focus on functionality and productivity. In recent years, that's been flipped on its head. While historic tech giants like IBM, HP and SUN focused on the business markets first, the new-age tech goliaths such as Google and Facebook began at the totally opposite end of the market – directly with the consumer – and are now disrupting the way businesses do business. Amazon is another great example. These guys started with an e-commerce book solution for consumers and now utilize their massive IT infrastructure to compete with HP, IBM and others for B2B customers.

Now, you might be working in another industry that, on the surface, seems less revolutionary or less technological. Look again. I would argue that, regardless of which sector you work in, pretty much every business decision in every industry drives a digital response. Technology – and in particular software – is impacting every corner of every business right across the globe.

Quite simply, whatever country, industry, company and department you work in, technological transformation is coming for you (if it hasn't got you already). The rapid nature of technological transformation means that business change is a fast-paced, continuous challenge. It never stops.

That's why I'm writing this book now – to ensure that I don't forget the lessons, the mistakes, the tricks, the good, and the bad of how to successfully transform a business in the digital age.

I wrote this book while I was still in post as CEO of EE. While it was hard to find the time to do it, one of the people who motivated me to put my experience to paper told me not to wait until I retire because then it would be less interesting and meaningful for the reader. You do not want to hear about a successful business story a decade or two after it happened.

So, it's up to date and relevant – but it's not written by an academic. Nor is it written by Jack Welch. In fact, it is written by someone who worked in key positions at many businesses that have now vanished!

I have worked for great companies, but unfortunately, most of them were unable to change to a new model and meet that new competitive threat: sometimes because of a lack of vision, sometimes because of a lack of leadership, and sometimes because of executive apathy.

EE was the exception to the rule in my career. Its story is fresh, modern, compelling and unique – both in terms of the circumstances in which we found ourselves, and of the way we met the challenge. Some of the decisions we took went against the stated rules (I challenge you to find another book that advises you to invest in a new brand and a product that no one knows they want, when you already have two highly successful brands with fiercely loyal customers in the market). But I hope you'll see why we took those decisions, how we implemented them, and what the outcomes ultimately were.

Hopefully, you will learn something from my experiences. I hope you find it practical and honest, and that it highlights the failures and struggles as well as the successes.

Good businesses never stand still. They continue to change, to innovate, and to outperform. Indeed, as I finish this book, we at EE find ourselves in the middle of yet another major transformation. Having pioneered superfast 4G, created a new brand, restructured a business and delivered immense internal change, we are building on those pillars to move the profitability of the business upward. We are continually differentiating our products and evolving our pricing model to match the ferocious pace of change in the way our customers are using our product – the product of connectivity.

We continue to transform our hundreds of stores and numerous service centres to become best in class, up-skilling 10,000 front-line staff and moving millions of customer calls to the web. We're reducing key indirect costs, strengthening our product launch processes to make them more efficient for our business, and more effective for our customers.

EE still has a lot of change ahead. It is in the process of being brought into the BT family and becoming that company's business for its second foray into mobile. But, as I sit here today we have a new brand, a new culture, a new retail estate and a new network. We have a business with a better future than when we began.

Happy reading.

Olaf Swantee

Inspiration, inventors and innovation

I was obsessed with not getting trapped by DVDs the way AOL got trapped, the way Kodak did, the way Blockbuster did… every business we could think of died because they were too cautious.

REED HASTINGS, NETFLIX

In this first chapter, I'll be sharing my views on a number of different effective styles of leadership that have been employed by some of the most successful global business leaders who have led some of the most successful transformations. These are people who have personally inspired me and shaped my thinking throughout my career (later in the book we'll explore leadership styles – a crucial component of any successful business change).

I also focus on the importance of technology in every aspect of society. Clearly, this is a recurring theme in the book, as technology has become the main agent of change that sits at the heart of many major modern business transformations.

Towards the end of this chapter I'll give you a short insight into the history of the UK telecommunications market. I've included this last section to give you context and background to the transformation that was specific to EE.

Transformative leaders

I am inspired by many things – the people I work with, my family, my friends, other business leaders. But what really inspires me – and gets me out of bed in the morning – is 'the opportunity'. Every day, the opportunities are out there and all you have to do is find them. That's pretty exciting.

Having worked in the technology industry for the best part of three decades, I often challenge myself to think back to what life was like before the digital revolution. What vision and gumption the Internet pioneers must have had to imagine a world of bits and bytes – a world beyond the fixed-line voice-carrying cables of the time.

Sir Tim Berners-Lee saw 'the opportunity'. He saw the potential of a connected world, joining protocols and technologies together to create the web. The first website was built at CERN and put online in August 1991. It gave information about the new WWW project with the following explanation of what these humble pioneers were doing:

> The WorldWideWeb (W3) is a wide-area hypermedia information retrieval initiative aiming to give universal access to a large universe of documents.

It also explains how elements beyond text could work on the web: 'It can include graphics, video and sound, for example.'[1]

So, a group of pioneers saw the opportunity to create a new world – a virtual world – that lay beyond the physical, where people could do more, learn more and trade more. Global businesses have been built from the web. Individuals have educated and bettered themselves. The previously unconnected now have access to a world that had been closed to them.

That's pretty inspiring. And it began with an opportunity.

Connectivity has accelerated economic development. It has enabled local entrepreneurs (wherever local is to them) to access knowledge, suppliers, and customers globally. It has, through its ability to harness instant global support, accelerated the demise of terrible political dictatorships. Equally, it has delivered a global audience for a new modern age of terrorism.

Yuval Noah Harari says in his excellent book *Sapiens* that, 'Over the last two centuries, the pace of change became so quick that the social order acquired a dynamic and malleable nature.' He explains: 'Today, even a thirty-year-old can honestly tell disbelieving teenagers: "When I was young, the world was completely different". The Internet, for example, came into wide usage only in the early 1990s, hardly 20 years ago. Today we cannot imagine the world without it.'[2]

In a world that's changing faster than ever before, strong leadership has never been more important.

There are many different styles of leadership. But good leaders all have one thing in common: they inspire people to do great things, and to find that opportunity. Through their inspirational leadership, they enable their people to do things they thought they were not capable of – and the technology industry has produced some of the world's most famous and enigmatic business leaders of recent times.

Bill Gates: 'think big'

I've never worked for Bill Gates, but I did have the opportunity to meet him at a dinner some years back. One of the richest men in the world – and one of the most successful business leaders in history – his is a truly inspirational story... the kid in the garage who built Microsoft from scratch.

He's worth billions of dollars – more than the GDP of many countries – and could rest easy knowing his achievements, riches and rewards are the signposts of his success.

But, after all he's achieved, does a man like Bill Gates rest easy? No. Having created and led one of the world's most successful companies, what does he do? He goes out to try to save the world. Because Bill Gates doesn't do small. He thinks big. He wants to solve the impossible problems.

That was the first lesson he shared with us at dinner: 'Trying to change things takes something big.' The second lesson he shared was around defining what you do – and how you measure it – with absolute clarity.

Bill Gates has taken the lessons he's learned in business and applied them to saving the world. He has examined – and challenged –

his own ambition. Gates looked at a global issue – poverty – and ascribed the fundamental problems it causes for those affected, namely poor life expectancy due to a lack of food and medicine.

He looked at the statistics and set a vision. He learned that in the 1960s, 18 per cent of people categorized in the world's lower income bracket died before they were five years old.

That number is now below 5 per cent. So, here in 2016, less than 5 per cent of people within the world's lower income populations die before they are five years old. He has now set himself a target of reducing that to 1.6 per cent by 2035 – the same life expectancy of an under-five-year-old in the United States during the 1980s.

He then set about planning how to reduce the impact of poverty and health issues for these people. He set targets around reducing key diseases such as smallpox, polio and malaria – diseases that kill millions of children every year.

Gates defined the problem, broke it down, simplified it, and set clear targets in order to try to eradicate these horrible diseases and drive life expectancy up.

That's clear, simple leadership.

The third lesson I learned from Bill Gates was about the importance of optimism. It was a striking reminder about the can-do power of positivity. He demonstrated throughout the evening that the human race is making significant progress and will be able to one day eliminate poverty. In fact we are eliminating poverty, but most of us are simply unable to see the progress we are making. We're just too close to the moment we operate in to understand all the positive things that are happening. Yes, we take a hit now and again, but we are progressing in the global fight against poverty. Knowing what we've achieved should give us the confidence and optimism to progress even further.

Gates demonstrates incredibly important leadership skills. He is optimistic and sees the glass as half full. He focuses on the opportunity, not just the risk. He has charisma and the drive to think big. He has always set a real and exciting purpose for the employees in his organization, but then takes the time to truly establish achievable, measurable but challenging goals and to define the key projects on the way.

Mark Hurd: 'the discipline of getting things done'

Another leader who has influenced me is Mark Hurd. He was the CEO at Hewlett-Packard, the company where I was working at the turn of the century.

Mark was an exceptional leader. He is an individual whose strength lies in powerfully driving execution. Mark taught me the discipline of getting things done. He delivered increased profits for HP for 22 straight quarters – without missing a single one. That's 22 quarters in a row – and the stock price more than doubled!

He achieved this because he was fixated on executing his plan throughout every corner of the business.

I've learned from that – first hand – and that is how I drive my business. Mark would focus on the numbers. He would review progress rigorously through clear dashboards. He would simplify issues. He would set real clear priorities and focus the business on its core assets and capabilities. He would deep-dive into problem areas. He would engage with all key managers in the business, not just the top team. Perhaps you already do these things in your business – I hope you do. Mark taught me how to perfect this leadership style and how to go deep into your organization as a leader without removing accountability.

In essence, he taught me that every successful business leader (whether the founder of a small startup, the CEO of a large global company, or somewhere in between) has to understand, monitor and influence the company's 'machine room' – its operations and those areas that require significant change. He also taught me that whatever your long-term strategy may be, success comes from the discipline of getting things done. Quite simply, you cannot transform your business without hitting your targets day in and day out. Perfect execution requires you to be constantly sharp and constantly focused.

Transformative technologies

Bill Gates and Mark Hurd are very successful, but very different leaders.

However, their careers share a commonality. They both led huge businesses within the technology industry – an industry that is in a constant state of transformation and in turn is constantly transforming our world.

'Moore's law' is a term first coined in the 1970s. It is an observation that is used to show just how rapidly technology is changing. Specifically, it suggests that 'processor speeds or overall processing power for computers will double every two years'.[3]

Essentially, due to the incredible unstoppable march of technology, computers and computing power will continue to progress exponentially in the years to come. And that means change. Change for countries. Change for societies. Change for governments. Change for individuals. Change for organizations.

In fact, more than any other, technology products are transforming our world in the most extraordinary way.

The rise of technology

Think back over your lifetime. Just 15 years ago, if someone had said that soon it would be impossible to be lost wherever you were in the world, you'd have thought they were mad. But, with the advent of satellite mapping, Internet giants like Google, product and software developers such as Garmin, and the rise of near-universal connectivity, it is now fact. Assuming you have the kit, it is now impossible to get lost on planet Earth.

Now think of the impact that has on the traditional map manufacturers. I'll place a bet that sales of atlases and pocket maps are at an all-time low. What about the impact it has on the holiday market? Just sitting here in my front room in London, I can now access the details of every coffee shop in Abu Dhabi (there are around 250 by the way) and I can find out whether Cairo has a zoo (it does – and a specialist fish garden).

And what about ourselves? How has this significant invention – one of many since the turn of the millennium – changed us as people? It's a fantastic thing that we are now able to find anything, anywhere, instantly. But over generations, it will also no doubt affect our innate directional skills honed over millions of years as trackers and hunters.

What about our societies? Geo-mapping and Internet technologies have made the world a smaller place, but have also sped up globalization, with societies blurring and blending into one another at a rate previously unseen in human history.

Quite simply, modern technology is changing our world – and everything within it – just as the wheel, the printing press, and the first airliners did.

The globalization and digitalization of our world means that new economies are emerging, new opportunities are arising, and new dangers are presenting themselves at the door of once untouchable titans of business. Consider the impact of Amazon on Walmart, which for many years was the world's largest company. And what about one of today's largest and richest companies? Apple moved into mobile and drove market leaders Nokia from a +40 per cent market share in 2008 to less than 5 per cent by 2013.[4] Open source software like Linux drove SCO Unix and Novell Netware out of the operating system market. The likes of Netflix sent high street video rental stores like Blockbuster down the pan. Spotify pushed everyone towards music streaming. And my old firm Orange is moving into mobile banking and microinsurance. I could go on and on. Every business in every industry is being impacted. The economic and industrial rulebook of the last 250 years, where the West led and the rest followed, is being ripped up and re-written.

It means that leaders will need to change the way they manage and inspire their businesses and employees. The next generation of leadership will change the shape of industries across the world, and the rise of the digital native will change the face, culture and expectations of the boardroom and your business. If leaders do not understand the risks and opportunities of technology for their business, their company will suffer. You cannot delegate this to the IT department. The potential benefits in productivity, in competitive advantage, and the risks of a Google-esque disruptor in your industry requires a business leader to be fully aware, informed, active and up to date in the modern, ever-changing world of technology.

And within that world of technology, no other element has had as much impact on our world as connectivity.

The importance of connectivity

Connectivity is the oxygen of technology. It turns a dumb device into a smartphone. It takes a slab of glass and plastic and transforms it into a magical black box that can transport your voice or image thousands of miles across the world in a flash. It can give you access to a world of information, entertainment and inspiration that was previously inaccessible. And with mobility, a whole new phase of connectivity is changing our world once again.

Generation M – the mobile generation who have never known a world without access to whatever or whoever they need, whenever they want or wherever they are – are coming of age. Their expectations and abilities, naturally honed through years of living in the mobile age, will shape our world in incredible and unexpected ways. Over the next decade they will become the dominant part of your workforce.

As a modern leader you must embrace technology. Your customers do, and your organization depends on it day in and day out. Do not delegate it to the IT back office team. Make it *your* business as the leader. Make sure that technology is aligned and utilized by each area in your company. Do not treat IT as a cost centre. In every business it has the potential to become a profit centre, a foundation for competitive differentiation. You also need to understand which companies are around the corner and fundamentally threatening the cost, the product and the routes to market in your business model by using unique software and hardware. Do not let your business become the next Nokia mobile phone.

A transformative telecoms market

For the last quarter of a century, the British mobile telecommunications market itself has been in a state of perpetual flux. In fact, I can't think of another single industry that has seen so much change.

Most of the network operators have either *owned,* been owned *by,* or forged strategic alliances *with* each other. This means that brands and businesses have come, gone or been actively evolved in unprecedented ways.

The reason for this significant level of fast-paced change is that the industry itself is at the bleeding edge of innovation and the technological transformation of our modern society. This is mainly due to the rapid growth of Internet access and the adoption of video and TV-based content.

At the same time, the device landscape is constantly evolving. Where we once used to have the big grey personal computer shackled to our desk at home, now, on average, we carry at least two Internet-hungry devices around with us on our person. Our devices are 'always on' – as are we.

Strategy analytics forecasts that we will hit 33 billion Internet devices worldwide by 2020, when the number of connections per person will more than double to 4.3.[5] So the industry has to deal with a potential doubling of telecommunications capacity every 12 months in a highly competitive market. This drives innovation and constant transformation.

Connectivity in society

Connectivity is now firmly cemented in the political agenda. It has become a general election pledge and a matter of key public importance. Connectivity – especially the lack of it – affects house prices, enables schools to boost their ratings and is now a reason to choose one coffee shop over another on the high street.

How things have changed.

Even as recently as the start of the 21st century, most local councils and communities would have protested against the installation of a telecoms mast or the disruption caused by the laying of fibre in the streets. But in under a decade – in Europe at least – a 360-degree shift has taken place.

So just how did connectivity move from being an enemy of the state to a fundamental human right in the space of just 10 years?

It all began back in the final decade of the 20th century, when a seismic shift occurred in the communications industry. The dominance of Vodafone Racal and British Telecom's BT Cellnet was, for the first time, challenged, with regulatory changes allowing new entrants into the market.

It opened up the opportunity for 'real people' to benefit from access to mobile communications technology for the first time. Prior to this, mobile phones – and the way you could buy them – were designed for the successful or aspiring businessman.

Indeed, in March 1984 when Vodafone was launched, the company positioned their service as being 'likely to find wide use among people constantly on the move, such as business executives, sales representatives, journalists, doctors and veterinary surgeons'.[6] In 1991, the Newbury-based firm became the first UK company to launch a GSM mobile phone service – the standard we still use today.

About 60 miles away in the heart of London, the UK's other mobile firm – Cellnet – was their only competition. Also having launched in the mid-1980s, Cellnet was the result of a 60:40 joint venture between British Telecom and Securicor.

This duopoly lasted almost a decade, and it wasn't until the launch of Hutchison Telecom's Orange and Mercury One2One that these two businesses were truly challenged.

Orange launched on 28 April 1994. It broke all the rules. No longer was the mobile phone market the bastion of sharp-suited executives and, forgive me, veterinary surgeons. The company extinguished the existing awkward way of buying a phone via resellers, and sold direct to the consumer with simple tariffs, easy-to-understand terms and a marketing campaign that was more art form than ad land.

Spearheaded by Hans Snook and his team of visionaries, they defined a market. Snook had, in fact, been sent from his bosses in Hong Kong to close down the company's ailing Rabbit service – a 'line-of-sight' mobile service in which you could only make calls when you could see a Rabbit symbol on a near-by building. This once-revolutionary idea had been quickly overtaken by the country's more adaptable, more flexible GSM services from the two established operators of Vodafone and Cellnet, and Rabbit did indeed cease trading in the early 1990s. But Snook saw an opportunity. With the UK Government looking to end the existing duopoly and encourage applications from businesses wishing to enter the mobile market, there was a chance to challenge the thriving Vodafone and Cellnet services with a simpler, more approachable and accessible service – a service that would be as appealing to the everyday man and woman on the street, just as Vodafone was to the ambitious executive.

Mercury One2One was the first of two companies to enter the UK market during the first half of the 1990s. Launching in 1993, the Mercury One2One team rolled out their network to cover the London M25 area, tempting consumers with free off-peak calls and other industry-leading offers.

Along with the affordable, straightforward and friendly proposition offered by Orange when Snook's team launched a few months later, anyone could now own a mobile phone. It sparked a boom for an industry and individual consumers that we still see the hallmarks of today.

In 1993, there were approximately 34 million mobile subscriptions worldwide. Nine years later, we passed the first billion. In 2015 – with more than 7 billion active subscriptions – there are now more SIM cards on the planet than humans.[7]

The mobile Internet revolution

At this point in time, in the final decade of the 20th century, mobile phones were used to make phone calls, and that was pretty much it. Text messaging followed in the late 1990s, and for some time calls and texts were pretty much it. But there was a bigger vision being hatched: the vision of a mobile Internet. The challenge was how to take the invention of Tim Berners-Lee and his colleagues, and put it in the pocket of every person in the country – and ultimately every person on the planet.

Having access to all the information and entertainment you want at the touch of a button, wherever you are, is the norm today, certainly in the Western world. However, at the turn of the millennium it remained the stuff of science fiction. Google was still a Stanford PhD research project. Facebook founder Mark Zuckerberg was still at high school, yet to hit Harvard and inadvertently create the social phenomenon of our age. YouTube was half a decade away from being registered as a URL, let alone having its first video uploaded by its founders at San Diego Zoo.

Printed newspapers were still a thriving business. They were *the* place to get your information from. Aside from 24-hour news and the advent of colour, television hadn't changed much since it became a publicly accessible service in the 1950s. Radio was still FM, and your choice of show was very much still dictated to you by the schedulers.

This was a time when people still saw the web as a thing for the nerds and the geeks. The dream of every home having a computer was still just that – a dream. Apple had just launched the iMac and computer PC prices were starting to fall, but many people still did not have their own computer, and would use the machines in their public library, school or university for not much more than word processing.

In spite of Vodafone's mid-1980s assertion, most journalists still filed their stories from telephone boxes on the street, and as for the vets, well, I have no clear information on that.

But things were about to change. The geeks were about to, if not inherit, then bear significant influence on, the Earth.

The first decade of the new millennium would see huge cultural, global and societal shifts, many of which were caused or fuelled by technology, and specifically connectivity.

The phone becomes 'smart'

Over the following 15 years, many behaviours, attitudes and social norms changed in the UK due to the rise of mobile. Cameras were integrated into phones.[8] Third-generation networks were launched. The first applications of news, weather and games began to appear on our screens. Many people purchased their first mobile – some for work, some for convenience, some for the glove box, some just to fit in. Prices fell both of handsets and cost of use.[9] Wireless computing hit our homes, followed by the pocket device with connected PDAs (personal digital assistants) and smartphones offering e-mail and limited Internet access. The iPhone launched, changing the fortunes of Apple and, arguably the industry, making the idea of the smartphone both appealing and desirable. Tablets made sofa surfing a reality, and video and TV appeared on the mobile. But it wasn't until the launch of 4G – the fourth-generation mobile networks enabling superfast broadband speeds on the move – that all these things came together to fulfil the promise of a truly social, mobile world where you really could access what you want, when you wanted, wherever you were. More of that later.

Within the industry, things changed dramatically too. Hutchison sold Orange to Mannesmann. Vodafone then merged with Mannesmann, which led to the sale of Orange to France Telecom. Former Orange owners Hutchison would then come back into the UK market with Three, a new challenger brand. Cellnet was wholly bought by British Telecom and ultimately re-branded as BT Cellnet, before being spun off as O2, and subsequently purchased by the Spanish firm Telefónica. Mercury One2One ultimately dropped the Mercury, and One2One was then sold to Deutsche Telekom and re-branded T-Mobile. All that happened within the space of five years.

Soon after, we would witness the meteoric rises and painful falls of Nokia, Blackberry and Motorola. Microsoft launched its first foray into mobile, but was swiftly overtaken by sleeker, sexier Apple products. Networks progressed through numerous standards – from 2G to 3G to 4G, with many incremental steps in between.

So, as you can see, an entire book could be written about the machinations, ambitions and effects of the mobile telecoms market in the UK in the 20th and 21st centuries. I give you this context as it's important to understand how EE came to be – and how corporate transformation is a constant in industries, companies and brands right across the business spectrum.

Technological change and in particular the digital and mobile Internet revolution will have a profound impact on every business and on every leader.

Now is a good time to ask yourself whether you have understood, embraced or anticipated the technological impact on your business and your leadership style.

Take the opportunity to learn from leaders in all kinds of businesses by observing their approach to securing transformation.

How do they establish the motivation for an organization to change? What goals do they set? Why are you inspired by them? Can you mirror their approach?

I learned from Bill Gates, Mark Hurd and many others. Who have you learned from? What did they teach you, and how do you apply those lessons to your everyday business life?

Sleeping with the enemy 02

Not all joint ventures fall apart... but failure is far from a rare occurrence. When we interviewed senior joint venture practitioners... they estimated that as many as 40 to 60 per cent of their completed JVs have underperformed or failed outright.
MCKINSEY & COMPANY

This chapter will give you a clear introduction and background to the incubation of EE. It will give you an insight into what happened behind the scenes to orchestrate one of the largest deals in the telecommunications market. Deals are always a 'win–win' on paper. However, one of the most challenging operational phases in a large transaction is immediately after the ink is dry and the champagne bottle is empty. It's not the popped corks that you'll be tripping over. In fact, the hangover strikes when the two parties have to wait for the necessary regulatory and competition approvals. You will read about this difficult phase in the 'integration planning' section, and hopefully pick up the good and the bad examples that we uncovered while bringing two giant businesses together.

Genesis of the joint venture

By 2009, Orange was the rising star of the UK telecoms market. It had seen some difficult times over the past decade, being owned and sold by a number of suitors before France Telecom took control and harnessed the potential of the Orange brand to create a European powerhouse, re-branding their assets across the continent with that famous coloured square and the ethos and values it imbued. Former BT Cellnet director and Virgin Mobile founder Tom Alexander had taken the reins of the UK business in 2008, propelling the company even further, and injecting a new sense of energy and enthusiasm. At the time, I was responsible for Orange's European operations, making sure that we were a lean, cohesive and focused business. Tom and I worked closely on repositioning the UK business, and over the space of 18 months, Orange UK moved from third place in the market (in terms of customer numbers and revenue), and was on the cusp of overtaking Vodafone to become the market's number two operator.

At the same point in time, T-Mobile was in a tough place. The brand was less potent than its rivals, the business was struggling to cut through, and the company was in need of a drastic re-shape. Its German owners brought in Richard Moat to run the UK business and instill a turnaround plan and mentality to boost both the company's profitability and its standing in the market. Like Tom, Richard is a seasoned telecoms professional, having cut his teeth in the early days of Orange, where he was the finance director for the business. He was the right man to bring in to turn the business around.

But both Tom's and Richard's turnaround plans were dealt a surprising hand when the French and Germans masterminded a new approach to the UK market.

What the two European teams were contemplating had never been done before in the telecoms market. Take two big, well-established, multi-billion-pound businesses that occupy the third and fourth positions in the market, push them together and create a single entity that automatically becomes the number one – in scale at least – overnight.

The joint venture was months in the planning. It was the secret brainchild of only a select group of people within the leadership teams of the French and German businesses. But, like all complex business deals, getting it across the line went right down to the wire.

A Franco-German adventure

The two teams, the French and the Germans, camped out at the Metropolitan Hotel in Mayfair, London – neutral territory – to iron out the final minutiae of the deal. Security guards flanked the lifts and key doorways as the teams of strategists, business chiefs and, of course, lawyers beavered away in separate rooms.

The challenge had been set to finalize the deal prior to the opening of the European stock exchanges early on the morning of 8 September 2009 – 36 hours away. Not easy at the best of times, but when you're dealing with your arch competitor, the restrictions on what you can say, share or sign, make things even tougher.

The teams engaged under strict rules, conscious that the deal had not yet been done and that loose lips here and there, or the wrong word or information given in passing, would not only be bad for business with the potential to sink the whole deal – but also down-right illegal.

While runners were frantically racing up and down corridors with papers to share and sign, inside the rooms of the Met, the teams were tiptoeing around highly complex subjects, aware that the wrong word out of place would kill this plan stone dead.

It was like introducing two highly combustible chemical components to each other – the wrong contact at the wrong time could send the whole thing up.

As the clock ticked on, more teams from the operational UK businesses were brought in on what had become Europe's biggest business secret. Eyes widened and jaws dropped as new initiates from the HR, procurement and communications teams were inducted into the secret. It was the first sight we had of just how impactful the news was to be to the existing Orange and T-Mobile UK teams when it hit their desks in just a few hours' time.

This was culture shock of the highest order. Over time, we would be asking teams comprising tens of thousands of people – former sworn enemies – to work as one and, together, build a business that challenged the status quo. We would be asking them to create a business that would become number one for revenue, achieve its synergy savings, grow its operating cash flow by nearly 12 per cent every year, and improve its profitability by at least 35 to 25 per cent EBITDA.[10]

The percentage of joint ventures that fail far outweighs those that succeed. Cultural problems are a key issue cited. In my experience, the destabilization of a business – and its people – while going through a joint venture is more significant than that of a business being bought. In a sale, it's crystal clear who the 'buyer' and who the 'bought' are. The complexities and nuances of a 50/50 joint venture are vastly more complicated as, for all the legal and contractual agreements, much is based on the personalities involved and the will of those who want to make it work.

The risks of forming a joint venture are high – as are the rewards. Our joint venture was developed to bring the power of two – the third and the fourth in the market – to create a number one, leapfrog the opposition and deliver an even better experience to UK customers.

The teams worked through many days and nights as the deadline loomed. But they did it. As most of London, Paris and Bonn slept, the 5th floor of the Met Hotel was alive with endeavour and ambition, touched with exhaustion and anticipation.

The big deal

On the morning of Tuesday 8 September 2009, the deal was announced to employees, analysts, the press and an unsuspecting industry. It was announced in that order and communicated with military precision. Telling your employees about something as significant as this is an essential part of leadership. It gives you a fighting chance of bringing people with you, inspiring them about the possibility, and above all showing them respect as part of the team that will be taking this forward.

With businesses the size, scale and geographical spread of both Orange and T-Mobile, it's almost impossible to get to everyone in the company instantly – even with the innovation of near-total connectivity. But the act of trying to do that is at least symbolic of a leadership style that is inclusive and respectful. While some may catch the news first on the web or the radio on their way into work, that e-mail, video message or invitation to join a call at least symbolizes your intent to inform first, and therefore your respect.

The ultimate concept of the joint venture was to create a new mobile champion for the UK. It was to be the clear market leader with the industry's leading revenue market share. It would have a management team committed to delivering market-leading profitability. It would be a company providing the most innovative services for UK consumers. And it would create significant value through the integration of the two businesses – up to £3.5 billion.

There were some key governance principles put in place to ensure joint control for the two businesses, with a streamlined decision-making process.

A board of directors was created with equal representation from France Telecom (FT) and Deutsche Telekom (DT). The board had two representatives from FT (one of whom was me), two from DT and two executive directors from the two UK businesses – Tom Alexander as CEO and Richard Moat as chief financial officer and deputy CEO.

The governance process was designed to allow the new company's management team to focus on running the business and its two brands, rather than shareholder discussions.

Dealing with the brands

The brands themselves were a subject of high speculation from day one. One of the key public milestones announced was that the T-Mobile and Orange brands would co-exist for at least 18 months in the UK, with a long-term brand strategy to be decided by the shareholders after this period. Press and employees speculated about what this could mean, but critically, the 28.4 million subscribers that the business now had, did not. The plan was to 'smart compete' for this period while the details of the future brand strategy were developed. It meant that Orange and T-Mobile would continue to deliver different propositions and exist in different ways, targeting different people in the market.

Unless you were an avid reader of the business or mobile trade press, you were unlikely to notice much change for the time being. But for those in the industry and those who watched closely from the outside, once the impact of the main news had been digested and died down, the questions came flooding in: Who will *really* be leading the company? How does an equal share joint venture work? Which brand will dominate? Does the word synergy really mean redundancy? And so on.

The journalists were keen to get their scoop, the analysts were keen to offer the smartest insight to their clients and the employees just wanted to know what the hell was going on.

In these situations, some of these questions can be answered, but some cannot. This is not because there is a desire to be evasive. There can be legal reasons, commercial reasons, or reasons of competition. It could also be that these issues at play just haven't been thrashed out yet.

As a leader, your job in these moments is to offer as much clarity as possible to help navigate the story and motivate the audiences in the right way. You have to both ride and face into the speculation. You have to over-communicate to employees, stamp on the inaccuracies and accept that the competition will enjoy their moment to criticize and scoff.

In the days that followed the announcement, our competitors took the position of welcoming the joint venture, stating that it would divert and distract the Orange and T-Mobile teams, allowing them to drive their own plans forward and continue to lead the market.

While at the time those statements made for good copy and may well have been the initial analysis from the teams in Newbury and Slough, history tells a different story. Often the battle of words is won in the long game.

As the competition were busy sending snappy soundbites over the media battle lines, our focus was on creating a long-term sustainable business – something that started with the development of our core corporate structure. If you structure the corporate core of a business incorrectly, there will be problems down the line. It means ensuring the right governance, the right transparency, the right respect, and the right team.

Here are six critical success factors that we put in place right at the start of the joint venture:

Ambition

Although there's a huge drive to deliver and over-succeed, do not underestimate the challenge. Sometimes a little conservatism goes a long way. Be realistic on the outcome when thinking about cost synergies, growth synergies and revenues. Often joint ventures fail because their ambition was too high.

Empowerment

When structuring a business, empowering the management team is absolutely key, right from the start. Our board of directors recognized that you cannot run a British company from Germany and France. It had to be run from the UK with clear reporting lines and responsibilities back to Bonn and Paris.

Transparency

A small board of directors (we had six) allows the development of a tight top team who should share the real challenges and goals with stark honesty. It is essential to have a team at the very top – and from the very start – that respects each other and is able to work together in an open and honest way.

Governance

While it's essential to put the traditional finance and audit committee structures in place, we found that limiting governance overload allowed real agility for our HQ team. Striking a balance of the required governance – while enabling the business to get on with the job in hand – is extremely important. There were only a few sub-committees, and the board of directors always tried to limit bureaucracy.

Decisions

With a 50/50 joint venture like ours, the shareholders and board of directors will have to accept that the JV CEO and CFO must act as the final decision makers for many issues. If the owners can't agree, let the CEO and CFO decide. In this model, it is important to have a strong CFO as well as a strong CEO, in order to maintain all of the necessary checks and balances.

(Continued)

Adopt and go

Because you are creating a new company, the tendency in a merger or a take-over is to rethink everything instead of picking between the two existing models. The 'adopt and go' model will force you to choose between the best individuals, the best IT stack and the best product set from both organizations. This allows you to gain time in integration and avoid losing critical know-how. It allows you to be nimble and move quickly. If you do it right, it will feel tough, as it sometimes means losing good people or expensive assets from your business.

Britain's biggest communications company

With the necessary due diligence completed, the joint venture was formalized some weeks later, in November of 2009. Having successfully got over the line and announced the JV, the hard work really began. Getting this far was an achievement in itself, but it was hardly even the start.

In fact, in the analogy of a rowing race, this was the equivalent of a two-man rowing team agreeing to get in the boat together. The starting gun had yet to be fired. The next two significant hurdles were formalizing the joint venture, gaining approval from the regulator and then operationalizing this huge endeavour.

While many suggested that the regulatory process would be a time-consuming distraction that would avert the Orange and T-Mobile teams from the day job, it came faster than many expected. Competition in the UK market was strong and vibrant and the firm belief among the shareholders and their teams was that the UK would be more competitive than most other European markets after the consolidation of the two businesses. The amount UK consumers were paying for mobile contracts was falling rapidly. Between 2006 and 2009, contract prices had fallen by 20 per cent, and the price per minute paid by consumers had fallen by 38 per cent.[11]

The UK's Office of Fair Trading had reviewed the situation before passing the power of veto to the European Competition Commission in the run-up to Christmas of 2009, and as the regulatory timeline ticked on, planning the operationalization of the joint venture was a task set for a small and focused set of teams.

Integration planning

Those first few months of 2010 were nervous times for the teams, planning well ahead for a business that didn't yet exist and, moreover didn't have the approval to exist.

Individuals from both T-Mobile and Orange were removed from the two businesses and set to work in 'clean room' groups aligned to their functional expertise – HR, Marketing, Legal, Procurement and so on. This meant they were no longer considered a part of their former businesses, and held a privileged position in planning the next steps of the new entity.

It was particularly tough as the scrutiny of the regulator was well and truly on them. Quite simply, until the joint venture achieved approval from the European Commission (and potentially the Office of Fair Trading), T-Mobile and Orange had to continue to compete against each other and could not operationally implement any element of the merger. You are not allowed to cooperate in commercially sensitive areas like pricing, product roadmaps, account management, etc. Generally, you are allowed to 'plan' the integration but not to 'do' anything until you have the final approval. This limits your work significantly.

'Clean rooms' are a risky business for those involved. If the joint venture succeeds, then fine. If it collapses, though, you're potentially unable to head back to your former business, depending on the information you've been party to. However, typically, even the 'clean room' teams and people who plan the integration have to abide by very strict rules such as:

- You must limit the scope of sharing any sensitive information to the individuals responsible for integration planning activities only.

- You must not share or discuss any customer/product-specific information, existing or future pricing or products, pending customer proposals or similar competitively sensitive information.

- Aggregated, non-customer/product-specific information can be shared, but only if you cannot discern information relating to specific products or customers.

(Continued)

- Any commercially or competitively sensitive information must be ring-fenced and you must ensure that it cannot be used in the usual course of business by either party for any other commercial purpose.
- You must not coordinate sales or market models, only make preparations.
- With retail, you can identify overlaps, footprints, space; but you must not share detail of sales volumes.

Clearly, every merger or take-over is different. So take the quote from the Orange and T-Mobile legal integration team into account. They told our teams, 'If in doubt, ask a lawyer... we are your friends' (surely the first time those words had ever been committed to print)!

The integration planning phase requires a tremendous amount of legal oversight and control whether you like it or not. There are no nods, winks or secret codes allowed – it must be played by the book, with assumptions driving many of the early key decisions.

Keeping 'business as usual' rolling

The challenge of integration is not just focused on the new entity – it's critical that you keep your momentum and focus on the existing business. That's a truly tough task, as everyone knows that the future will be different and people are drawn like magpies to the new world. For those not involved in creating the new entity – those who are left to run the existing business – this can create significant de-motivation and uncertainty, which in turn can put the potential of your future plans at risk.

The story of EE is bookended by huge integration challenges. The first, we're reading about now – the pulling together of Orange and T-Mobile... the businesses that would become EE. It was a tough period for those involved, and very unsettling for many employees. Employee motivation was at an all-time low, and the future seemed unclear.

However, in the final chapter of this book, you will read about BT's purchase of EE – yet *another* example of a challenging timeline for integration. In this case, it took more than a year between the moment that the shareholders agreed the deal and the deal being formally approved by the authorities. However, although the integration planning phase was long, in this case we managed to drive employee motivation *up*. *The Sunday Times* 100 Best Companies to Work For, which is an established, well-known, objective survey of employee motivation in the UK, featured EE in 7th position in 2015, marking EE's fourth appearance on the list and the company's highest ranking to date.

So, how do you maintain momentum and reduce de-motivation and uncertainty during an integration planning phase? What were our learnings from the Orange and T-Mobile merger, and how did we apply them to drive a better result during the integration of EE and BT?

- Demonstrate credibly and frequently to your employees that the new combined company builds on what exists today – it is an evolution of their work and a testimony to what has been delivered so far, not a wholesale reinvention.

- Limit the information about the integration planning activities to an absolute minimum until just a few weeks before the actual integration. It will always be incomplete and you will not be able to answer to the specific concerns of an individual employee anyway until you actively kick-start the integration work.

- If necessary, establish additional clear retention and performance award programmes for your critical performers.

- Ensure and communicate that any people selection will be fair, balanced and based on true performance. The current work of each individual will go a long way in defining her or his future.

- Stay focused yourself. People look at you and your top team. If you take your eye off the ball because you are insecure about your own future in the new entity, they will do the same. It is your responsibility to stay driven, even though you may be the first to lose your job.

The European Commission gave its approval to the joint venture of Orange and T-Mobile in the Spring of 2010, stating that the business would have to give up a chunk of its network spectrum to allay any anti-competition concerns. On 30 March 2010, the process went into overdrive. With approval given, the operationalization of the business would now need to be delivered. No more was this about theory, slide decks and proposals – the joint venture was now very much a reality.

From this date on, a whole new governance model came into play.

The UK Orange and T-Mobile teams were now able to share, cross-check and validate their work and all information necessary to organize the integration of the two companies.

The challenge of confidentiality was now at a shareholder, not an operational level. It meant that the 'JV company board' was now the top decision-making body for the joint venture, and represented both groups of shareholders. As well as making the decisions, the challenge of the JV company board was to ensure that confidential information about one parent company was not accessible to the other parent company.

The teams worked feverishly to build the processes and structures needed to bring the two businesses together, and on 11 May 2010, an official announcement was made, detailing the company's new team, vision, plans and name – Everything Everywhere.

Everything Everywhere: what's in a name?

More an ambition than a company title, Everything Everywhere was controversial to say the least. It was a bold promise that spoke of instant access to the people, places and things you wanted at the touch of a button. Arguably, with superfast fixed and mobile broadband accessible to over 80 per cent of the UK population, it's an ambition that is being fulfilled. At the time it was a 'Marmite' choice of a name – some loved it, some hated it – and much attention was poured onto it.

But behind the name was an equally bold business that the two teams had built.

Everything Everywhere was formally created on 1 July 2010 – one company, running two of Britain's most famous brands: Orange and T-Mobile.

It had plans for a single, super-network that would be bigger and better for customers.

It promised a boost for sales with the biggest telecoms retail presence in the UK, as well as the promise of brilliant service.

It revealed changes for its fixed-line broadband and business-to-business presence – two markets where Orange and T-Mobile had both under-delivered in the UK.

And it unveiled its new leadership team – one that, in these early days, was evenly made up from the old T-Mobile and Orange UK boardrooms to ensure stability and familiarity within the business.

The company had over 16,000 employees; head offices in Bristol, Hatfield and London; customer service centres in Darlington, North Tyneside, Plymouth, Doxford, Greenock and Merthyr Tydfil, and a combined total of 713 Orange and T-Mobile stores on the high streets of Britain.

In just nine months, a team of 100 people had taken two of the UK's best-known companies, pushed them together and created one of Britain's biggest businesses. Overnight, it had gone from a joint third and fourth in its market, to the leader in terms of revenue and customer numbers.

Internally, the mantra was simple: 'We've established ourselves as the number one, now we have to earn it.'

Most leaders are excited when the deal is signed. There is huge relief when a negotiation has concluded. Buying, selling and merging all start with a thrilling transaction. Unfortunately, the real success will often depend on what happens afterwards.

You have to ask how you can motivate yourself and the key managers to go through a legally and tightly controlled integration planning phase – one which may very well end up in the cancellation of the deal by the regulatory authorities.

You also need to think hard about how you can maintain momentum in your existing business while all this is happening. Be prepared to focus on the here and now as much as tomorrow – even when your own job is on the line, or when you're eager to start that new company. Without that strength and stability in your existing business, you risk the foundations of your future enterprise.

A new team to deliver

03

Coming together is a beginning. Keeping together is progress. Working together is success.

HENRY FORD, FORD MOTOR COMPANY

In this chapter, I want to share with you the key strategic asset that delivers true success to a business – its people. Making sure you have the right people, doing the right things, in the right place is essential to the long-term health of any business. Often this means making exceedingly tough and painful decisions upfront, and sometimes you lose good people in the process. But the over-arching objective is that you, as the leader of a business, need to ensure you have a team that's fit for the future, and that matches the ambition of the company itself. Here, I'll explain what we did at EE, and how we drove a consistent and coherent top-down approach in terms of structure, objectives and attitude.

A leadership structure to enable transformation

My elementary school maths teacher would have held his head in his hands if I'd told him that 3 + 4 = 1 but that's exactly what we had proved to be the case with the joint venture.

We had taken the two trailing businesses in their industry, put them together and created the leader. The question now was how do we sustain that leadership – not just for the year ahead, but for the long term? How do we become an industry leader that drives its own destiny?

That meant some tough decisions for many, both personally and professionally.

Between the official formation of Everything Everywhere on 1 July 2010 and the following summer, the leadership team had done a good job in stabilizing the business and its people. Both of the brands continued to perform well, with Orange nipping at the heels of Vodafone, and T-Mobile battling O2 with cheeky challenger advertising, its infamous flash-mobs and great offers.

Evolving our business

However, to move the company to the next stage of its plan, an evolution of the business was needed. Tom Alexander had completed his goal of bringing the two businesses together and leading not just Orange but the T-Mobile brand too. Richard Moat had also successfully managed the purse strings and the operational elements of this massive business, stabilizing the finances and performance of not just one super-tanker of a business, but two.

With both Tom and Richard leaving the business, I was asked, as one of the board directors of the joint venture, to lead the company through its next stage of transformation and operational execution as chief executive.

My first task was to build a new team, reducing what had become a leadership team that now looked out of proportion with where the business needed to go.

When I was asked to run the business, the organization was like Noah's Ark – there were two of everything. It was the result of two established businesses with two established leadership teams coming together and needing to maintain operational delivery and retain senior company knowledge. However, having two leaders responsible for HR, two for marketing, two for strategy, and so on, made it unwieldy, complex and inefficient. It made it impossible to do what needed to be done.

I decided to reduce the leadership team from 25 roles reporting to a CEO to 10. This resulted in a very tough selection process, and a lot of great people left the company. However, the fact was, that while the complicated merger structure did allow the company to maintain a lot of pre-merger know-how (something that was essential to maintain share and keep the ship sailing), it simply did not enable the transformation that was now required. We now needed to be nimble and move – fast.

I needed to accelerate the integration and the leadership plan. A smaller, more accountable structure helped to achieve this while also reducing costs.

My new leadership team structure was in place the first day I was in the office, but I had spent a lot of time defining it before that, creating some high-level organizational objectives and guiding principles.

Here are the organizational design principles we used for the restructure of EE's management team:

1 Streamline the top team.

2 Ensure appropriate top-line reports with increased commercial orientation.

3 Eliminate legacy product structures.

4 Increase commercial transparency and steering.

5 Provide clear focus on new propositions and customer end-to-end experience, and re-balance towards customer base and retention.

6 Merge sales and service functions to increase long-term loyalty and add service focus to the sales process (and vice versa).

7 Increase integrated technology transparency and leadership.

8 Maximize focus on data growth.

9 Eliminate duplication and merge middle-management functions.

10 Don't 'rock the boat' on units that work.

With these principles, we took a large team of executives and created a more nimble and accountable group of 10 – with a focus on not just managing a business, but transforming it to become an organization that could execute and deliver.

Mapping out the structure

So where do you begin when you need to build such a leadership structure? The most fundamental task should be to define what your desired profit and loss (P&L) structure is. A P&L structure defines how you want to report, manage and control your business. It helps you allocate and focus financial resources. It helps to identify and select which parts of the organization are cost centres and which are profit centres.

In defining your P&L structure, you need to ask yourself, do you want to create country P&Ls, consumer P&Ls, product and technology P&Ls, solution P&Ls or a combination of the above?

To answer that question, I outlined seven key areas that I considered as we moved toward the right answer – Time, Simplicity, Priorities, Functions, Size, Symbolism and Measurement.

Time

If you have to transform a company in a short period of time (ie in less than 24 months), it is unlikely you will have the luxury of creating, implementing and embedding new P&Ls. If this is the case, I recommend that you choose the P&L your existing systems can produce. This may sound obvious, but I have found that many times it contradicts your transformation objectives. For instance, if you find yourself leading a product-centric company that needs to become more focused on the end customer, it is logical to move to a business model where you measure financial results by customer segments rather than products. This will focus your organization on customer returns rather than pure product returns. The problem is often that you will need to change all your IT systems to move from a product to a customer P&L model, which is too costly and will take years to put in place. Previously I have worked in companies where we spent too much time establishing baselines and reports before we could move. If time is of the essence, then choose what's already available to you rather than trying to reinvent the wheel.

Simplicity

Try to avoid more than two versions of the 'truth'. Running a company with more than two P&Ls is extremely challenging and creates enormous complexity. Obviously, there are very large companies (IBM, GE and GM, for instance) that have grown to run on multiple P&L models over many years. In my experience, if you need to move quickly and run a company that is in difficulty, try to keep it really simple from a P&L perspective. Select one dominant model with a maximum of one overlay (for example, a country P&L with a product P&L overlay). With EE, we decided to stick to a simple product-based P&L view: one focused on the consumer and one focused on the business-to-business market. This avoided the need to introduce a new IT system but enabled us to focus on two distinct large customer groupings, each with its own product, pricing, and go-to-market strategy.

Priorities

I also mapped the P&Ls against two axes – relative market share and relative market growth rate.

The first axis gives an indication of the ability to generate a return. If you are number one or two in a market with high market share, you will typically generate a higher profit compared to being a small player.

The second axis will give you an indication of the future attractiveness of the market.

You essentially end up with four segments:

1 Low (or no) growth, but high relative market share. For example, Microsoft in the PC operating system market. Typically, businesses in this area are called 'cash cows' as they are very profitable and need to help to fund investments in segment 3 (below).

2 Low (or no) growth, but low relative market share. *The Independent* – the UK newspaper that recently stopped producing its daily print edition – would have been a candidate for this segment.

3 High growth but low relative market share. An example here would be Microsoft in the market for mobile operating systems. The businesses in this segment tend to be really strategic. They will need to carry the company in the future, when they can increase market share. Generally, you cannot afford to have too many businesses in this segment because they will require capital and their future is unclear.

4 High growth and high relative market share. Facebook in the market of social networks is a good example here. These are clearly the stars.

Each segment requires its own strategy. Structuring your business along these segments helps you to establish priority in your leadership structure.

So, map your businesses or your products in each of the segments. Make sure you do not have too many in segment 3 and limit investments of the ones in segment 2. Ideally, following my examples above, make sure that the same people do not manage businesses in different segments at the same time. Each segment requires its own unique management skills and focus.

I made that mistake at EE, asking one team to manage the multi-million Euro cash cow (a business with high relative market share, but low market growth) as well as a small but promising line of business (a business with low relative market share but high market growth).

The new business was a simple idea. If customers started using their phones like mini-computers, why not offer a suite of additional chargeable services such as installation, education, or fast-line access to the top technologists in the company who could solve complex customer issues. In the PC industry, these products are driving significant additional revenues. IBM turned these services into a multi-billion-dollar business. We asked 'what can we introduce to drive revenues and differentiation beyond our traditional service'?

What did the team do? They spent all their energy on the cash cow and not on the new potential growth business.

Why? Because the cash cow is traditional, while the new line of business was disruptive – and disruption means risk. Something that big businesses often don't cope well with.

Functions

The separation of operational and support functions is obviously quite important, but can slow your top team down. Operational units like responsibility for their own support functions and to drive them without too much discussion. My guiding principle is that if more than two organizational units need the same type of functional support and it is highly specialized (HR or Finance, for example), bundle that support to save cost and to attract the best specialized talents. In doing that, you need to make sure that these support teams treat the operational units as their customers. The operational units should have a strong say in their cost envelope and their service level targets.

Size

Try to keep the top team leaders to a maximum of 10. It is extremely hard to manage more if you want to create a team that will truly turn your company around. I had to remove 35 per cent of the management team on the day I started because I had way too many VPs stepping on each other's toes. You cannot manage transformation unless there is absolute clarity and simplicity in your top team structure. Too often, top structures become compromised because there are too many cooks in the kitchen. I always test the top structure with people outside the company and, importantly, my front-line staff – the people who speak to our customers every day. Do they understand immediately what one box means and what it is supposed to do? If not, you have your first blocking point in moving things forward. I like to work with boxes that people recognize instantly: sales, manufacturing, finance, people, marketing, and so on.

Symbolism

Sometimes you have to create a unit that symbolizes transformation in itself. If a company does not have a history of excellent execution, you may want to create a 'performance' box. One of the enablers for me that transformed EE into a fast-moving and highly credible business, was the creation of an entirely separate team focused on performance management, company integration, and transformation. This unit was responsible for immediately implementing a performance management system to clarify accountabilities that were linked to the company's objectives. This system helped us to sharpen execution through better priority setting, measurement and inter-departmental cooperation. It was also instrumental in driving the integration of legacy processes, systems, products, and tools. Merging and integrating is a core competency that typically sits better outside operational functions. The team also managed the 10 largest transformation projects, which cut across the company. More of that later.

Measurement

It is essential to define what each area's responsibilities are, and how you would measure their results at the highest and most granular levels. While you should build the key measurement principles for each department with each leader, having a consistent structure in place and a clear view of the accountabilities and responsibilities of each department is key.

In my experience, the exercise of building the correct, simple top structure requires you to test a few alternative structures. It is also key to understand the end-to-end, from-and-to picture and evaluate how hard is it to change to this new structure, how many successful teams have to be split up to deliver it, and which enterprise-wide processes will be severely impacted.

What is essential, however, is not to make the mistake I have made many times in the past. Do not start to compromise the integrity of the structure because of the great people you find or you know. These people, obviously and rightly, have career and job expectations and leaders tend to consider building structures that accommodate the aspirations of those excellent people in some way. You have to minimize this classic mistake. Too many top teams are built around people and not around company objectives. I have always regretted compromising the top structure to accommodate the career or business aspirations of a strong individual. Yes, attracting and retaining talent is essential, but not at the expense of the right structure. If you weaken the integrity of the structure to appease the ambitions of the individual, you send a signal to the other members of the team that there is one person who is more important than the rest. He or she has a remit that has been tailor made. If you need a team to deliver true transformation in a business, finish defining your uncompromised top structure and then select your team of individuals.

I also recommend that you do not compromise structure because you don't want to 'upset' the organization and create too much change. If you need to fundamentally transform a company, you have to build an organization that enables a minimum of bureaucracy, while delivering maximum accountability that's aligned to your transformation objectives. You will upset the organization more if the re-organization of the business becomes an annual event because you didn't make the necessary tough changes first time around. A company and its organization require sustained periods of structural stability. I have made this mistake several times in my career and have had to re-align the structure of the team and undertake a small re-organization shortly after I had just implemented the new organization. This should be avoided. Go all the way and try to build the right organization and structure from the start.

Selecting a team to move the company forward

So, you have the structure and the boxes in the right place. Now you need to fill them. You cannot transform anything without selecting the right people for your team.

On my wall, I have a picture of the first team I managed. I was in my late 20s and the team was responsible for the development of the PC business at Digital Equipment in Europe, the Middle East and Africa. They consisted of an Egyptian former ballet dancer, a young Belgium woman, an experienced and older Swiss engineer, a Russian student, two experienced product managers, an American, an unusual Finn, and a hardworking smart cookie from Sri Lanka. When I look at the picture, the team looks like loose sand. Each member of the team was completely different from me and from each other. It meant that the team was fun, it was diverse, it was explosive, it was nearly impossible to manage the conflicts and the differences... it was one of the best teams I have ever had the honour to lead. I felt a real wrench when I had to move on to a job in the United States. I left one of the best teams behind.

Building a brilliant team

Building and running this team taught me a number of important lessons in people selection:

1 A high-performance team will be diverse in experience, gender, nationality, age, and background. The most important of these is gender diversity. Leadership teams with little or no gender diversity have less chance to drive success. I have come across many leaders who have limited gender diversity in their teams simply because the search company they were using did not find enough female candidates and picked the best of what they had from the male candidates available. This is astonishing when research shows that the financial gains for businesses are significant if a gender-diverse board is running the company.[12]

2 Select people not just by what they can do, but by their potential and their attitude to change. Too many leaders spend huge amounts of time in interviews digging through the details of a candidate's CV, finding out what that person has done in their past. What a CV doesn't tell you is what that person could deliver in future. In interviews, I try to discipline myself to spend no more than 50 per cent of my time on the CV, to allow enough time to focus on understanding the potential of an individual. Potential is primarily driven by the distance between the task and the person's comfort zone. I look at the things that drive their personality, such as their ability to learn, and their levels of curiosity, courage and energy. Big jobs require people with skills and experience, but people who have big jobs got there because they had the potential to stretch into something new and different. One of my top leaders at EE – our chief of technology – had never managed a telecommunications network. He used to work in IT and had become instrumental in building an international airport. With a great team below him, he transformed two under-performing mobile networks into the strongest in the UK. In the process, he established the world's fastest mobile network. All this in less than 18 months! During 2014, he was named Chief Technology Officer of the year. I appointed him because he had passion, an infectious energy and he had learned how to manage very large complex projects with multiple suppliers and employees.

3 Make sure that you select people who are interested in working as a team. It is really important to envision how top candidates will act and react with others in the team as one unit. Generally, you

can clearly spot the individuals who are interested in operating for themselves rather than the collective. They often come recommended and your executive search partner may push them hard as 'a real star'. Having met them, you may even rate that person highly. But do not look at them in isolation. Be strict with yourself and assess how they will operate with your other stars. Trust your intuition and role-play your first management meeting with that person in the room. How does it feel for you, for the others, for your future successor?

4 Secure some people who intimately know the company, the history, the cultural challenge, the operational and strategic plans. This is especially key when you are new to the firm, but it is also imperative for a company you are going to change quickly. While you do not want people who are stuck in the past, those who can help make sure that the new team learns from history are extremely useful. In general, I believe in a good mix of promoting people from within the business, hiring a number of people from outside of the business, and retaining a few existing proven leaders.

5 If you have already managed to establish some of your new company's values before you select your team, make sure that you test all candidates against them. You want a diverse team, but they must all be in line with the values. At EE I wanted my leaders to be bold, to be clear, and to be brilliant – these were the company values we ultimately established (see Chapter 6). If you have not defined these prior to developing your structure and your team, try to at least define one value that you judge as non-negotiable. Consistently test your candidates against this one value to avoid making big mistakes.

If you have to select external talent, try using simple methodologies to avoid mistakes. During interviews, I use the 'Five E' concept. I probe the CV and leverage references to identify **Experience** and **Education**. I look at body language and use it to try to identify **Energy** levels. The most difficult of the five Es to identify are **Empathy** and **Ethics**. These are the so-called soft factors and yet they are the most crucial. You do not want people in your team without these. Background and family can help you establish an opinion. I also enlist the help of the PAs, the receptionist and the security personnel to provide a view. These members of your support team are masters in recognizing the candidates who do not have these attributes. The candidate will probably demonstrate strong social skills to you but more important are the natural behaviours they exhibit when they sign in at the reception and when the secretary brings them to your office.

Transforming the management structure

Once you have your leadership team in place, it is important to develop the structure under them extremely quickly. Re-organizing companies creates uncertainty and doubt. Obviously, you first need human resources to map out the process, key principles, diversity targets, total full-time employee target numbers, number of contractors, and desired management structure.

Personally, I always try to keep management structures as flat as possible to avoid bureaucracy and unnecessary costs. Adding managers and management layers in a mature company undergoing transformation needs to be done purely from a zero-based budgeting perspective. Businesses can get fat and flabby if there is not rigorous and ongoing discipline baked into the structure. Unnecessary extra management layers and structures can creep in over time. If you want to drive a fast and successful transformation, keep your senior teams lean and focused, and secure the absolute minimum number of managers within the structure.

With more managers comes a greater risk of miscommunication. You must have played the game of Chinese Whispers when you were a child. You sit in a circle with your friends and the first person whispers a message into the ear of the next. Each child passes on the message by talking into the ear of the next person. The last person speaks up and explains what he heard. The more people you have in the circle, the higher the chance that the message is corrupted at the end. Management layers function in exactly the same way. The more layers you have, the more the risk that communication flows clog up and messages get lost.

The discipline of spans and layers

So, along with the span of control increase, you should also create a target for reducing layers of management within your organization. If you only set a target for one but not the other, managers simply shift around while the structure remains bloated.

The simplest approach is to take the existing ratios and give each of your direct reports a target for simplifying them.

At EE, it was even more important because of the Noah's Ark situation I mentioned earlier. We had two managers, not just in the leadership team, but in practically every area because the company was established out of a merger of two businesses with similar structures and operations. We tasked the organization with removing two layers of management and getting to a span of control of 10. This would effectively result in a 35 per cent reduction of overheads.

The principles we used at EE were as follows:

- Restructuring will focus on overhead roles and the back office, not on the 'front-line' service and sales forces.

- We will create a unified management structure and eliminate duplication in structures.

- Each business leader will be accountable for achieving team restructure targets.

- Each department will receive a dedicated person from the human resources department to secure coordination across the whole company and to manage the communication and cooperation with the works councils.

- Each business leader, in partnership with HR, will drive the selection process for their organization.

- Selections and reductions will be made using a common set of tools and according to a defined process.

- There will be stringent rules around building next-level teams.

- There must be clear diversity throughout the organization, zero tolerance on poaching from other departments and no 'bumping'.[13]

(Continued)

- We will use the opportunity to manage out low performers and improve high-cost/low-productivity areas.
- We will work hard to avoid loss of key talent or high performers wherever possible.
- We will insist on there being no disruption of business-critical processes or projects.
- We will have clear and consistent orchestrated communication to employees and external parties.

Having a limited number of management layers and a good average number of employees reporting to each manager means you can speed up decision making and better empower people at all levels of the business. Plus, if you have an average of 10 people reporting to one manager, you make sure that each manager really needs to manage rather than constantly *do*. They will be focused on coaching, delegating, training, guiding, motivating and developing their team. They do not have the time to micro-manage if they want to be effective and succeed within the organization. The average of 10 is a good guiding principle. Sales and service organizations tend to have wider spans of control and specialized teams such as technology and marketing tend to be a little smaller.

Driving wider spans of control for a smaller management community means that the people closest to the customers feel that the distance between them and the leadership team has reduced, giving them better line of sight and a feeling of being closer to the top of the house. Of course, conversely, managers – and people who want to become managers – will have fewer opportunities to move up, so you have to find the right balance for your organization.

Regardless of the balance you hit upon, you will have a lot of resistance and your management community will claim that it is impossible to run the business with fewer layers and a wider span of control.

It is always possible.

Once you have the right structure for your business, each of your direct reports should be tasked with developing a simple plan of their area that should include the objectives of their organization, structure and interdependencies with other organizations. After the approval of these individual plans, the leadership team can execute them and secure their management selection.

At EE, we delivered this huge task in just three months. The structure was simpler, faster, and we secured the best leaders. In parallel to this work, we implemented an end-to-end performance management system, which helped to accelerate change by reducing inefficiencies. It is important to execute this in parallel with the creation of a new organization because it helps to establish a better structure. You win time, and it forces the management structure to anchor and clarify inter-dependencies. We will cover the performance management system in Chapter 5.

Establishing priorities

The trusted SWOT analysis has stood businesses in good stead for years, and sure enough, this is where we began in the creation of the key priorities of EE. You should always start by understanding your strengths, weaknesses, opportunities, and threats. Map them out on a piece of paper but keep the process simple and clear. Build a list of priorities that are direct, meaningful and relevant to your challenge. If you don't remember what you wrote down, your list is too long. If the list has only words and no numbers, try again!

Test the priorities with people at all levels of the business – not just the management community. Go to the people in your business who do not have a hidden agenda. They sit in your call centres. They work in your stores. They deal with your customers every day. They are the front line. They are the key to transformation. They will tell it to you straight and help guide you and your key priorities. As a CEO, you cannot spend enough time with them. If ever I am in doubt about the priorities, I go back to these people – the true voice of the organization.

I cannot overstate just how important it is for a CEO to listen to and be led by the front line in the early stages, and right through your tenure. When I draw my organization, I do so as an upside-down triangle – a pyramid on its tip. The front line dominates the broad base of the pyramid at the top, and I sit at the bottom by the tip of the pyramid. It is both a symbol and reminder that helps me be clearer about the SWOT, priorities and execution.

A new leadership style for a new business

When you have clarity on the fundamental priorities of your business, organize employee sessions to test them out, and use them to begin establishing your style. It is really important that you define your leadership style right from the start. Your style will be essential in how you want the company to achieve its transformation goals.

At EE, I needed to show that we required tremendous speed in execution. It was all about how we accelerated the execution of company plans rather than reinventing a strategy. So during my first employee sessions, I demonstrated that I listened but that I was impatient and eager to move on.

I also tried to set examples.

There were two months between me being announced as the new CEO and actually starting in the job. From the moment the announcement was made, I noticed that the employees were sceptical about my ability to drive the necessary change. They had seen and heard it all before. They had seen management teams talk the right talk, but not always deliver. I realized that I had to show them a new way. I had to show what 'acceleration of plans' meant. I had to show true execution.

I decided to skip the tried and tested 'first 90 days' as a CEO, and I promised them that I would have my new management team in place on day one – my first day in the office.

Few people believed I would do it. Unfortunately for my wife, she believed it all too readily. She was upset because it meant that I had to finish my old job, as well as decide on and appoint the new team during a long-awaited family vacation in Denmark. I also decided to try to resolve a major dispute with a key supplier during this time. This company was delaying our ability to drive a long-awaited integration of our two networks into a better, stronger and more affordable one. It meant hours of calls, meetings, debates and decisions. We had to do all of this during a total of six weeks in the summer of 2011. And all it did in Denmark was rain.

But once in London, with my feet under the desk, it allowed me to spend the first true employee session on my very first day to announce my new 35 per cent smaller leadership team. I had kept a promise and delivered a fantastic new leadership team to the company. Half of the team was made up of new faces, and it was smaller to ensure less bureaucracy, better teamwork, and superb operational excellence. It gave the business a boost from day one.

During the session, I asked the employees what the other key issues I had to address were. Several said that we needed to finally resolve the conflicts with our strategic partner – the one that had delayed network integration for several quarters. They asked me when this would be fixed. I said, 'in two weeks'. Again, a lot of people did not believe that this was possible as the business had been trying to do it for 18 months. But, sure enough, we settled our issue out of court and were able to announce it in time to prove that from that point on we were going to set highly ambitious deadlines and deliver on them. Looking back, I'd say we managed to deliver on these deadlines 90 per cent of the time. From the start, this helped to establish a 'can-do' attitude within the business, and gave me the credibility to insist on the same behaviour from the rest of the company at all levels.

Different leaders have different styles

Establish your style quickly, but make sure that it's compatible with what's required to achieve transformation.

During my career, I have used various styles at different points in time depending on the environment, on the changes required, and on the existing or new culture we needed to introduce.

There are many different styles. Each leader will clearly have a mix with one or two accentuated attributes. Your functional background will be the first defining factor. Someone with a predominant financial background will probably act and certainly be perceived differently to the leader who comes out of engineering or sales. The way you tend to interact with others is the second key defining area. Are you a team player? Are you approachable for people? Are you consensus oriented or autocratic with others?

Remember, your people will listen to what you have to say, but they will also look at how you act and react. They may not like how you do things but they will at least understand what you expect from them.

Whether you want them to or not, your employees will decide consciously or unconsciously about your leadership style early on. The first impressions you make are key and are difficult to amend later on.

Above all, credibility is key. While a good transformation leader has certain 'chameleon' capabilities, being an authentic leader – whatever your style – is a must. If you do not display authenticity, your credibility as a leader will fail.

Personally, I believe that some of the key leadership style attributes that enable company-wide transformation are:

- Be optimistic with a focus on the future. I spend hardly any time talking about the past.

- Encourage teamwork and consensus, but with a bias for action.

- Be ambitious and bold – set the bar high and work your socks off.

- Use target numbers wherever possible. Words alone can confuse transformation.

- Be really clear, repeating priorities and expectations everywhere all the time. If you are getting bored hearing your own words, then that's good – your people are now probably starting to listen and understand your plans.

- Focus more on the how and less on the what. This is execution.

- Be impatient, but avoid shooting from the hip.

- Establish true empowerment, but challenge everyone in the company at all levels. If you are the leader, you can by-pass everyone in your organization to understand, to motivate, to push and to challenge. Never remove accountability in the hierarchy but go as deep as you can to inspire and challenge.

Ultimately, there is no right or wrong. You need to develop your own style and turn the volume up and down on various nuances depending on the situation your business is in and how you plan to motivate your people.

At EE, once we had launched a new network, new 4G-based price plans and handsets, hundreds of revamped retail stores, and a new marketing campaign, I spent a lot of time emphasizing the importance of customer-centricity and the front line. This was an area where

I turned up the volume for my leadership style – it helped me to drive even more focus on improving a new customer experience, a new way of selling, and amending customer processes that were wrong.

People are at the heart of any successful transformation – you, your team and the business at large. When building a new team, first define whether your structure is efficient. Most organizations and structures tend to grow out of proportion over time. Consider the opportunity to simplify, clarify and de-clutter your structure, making sure you select compatible people who live the values and ambition of your new company.

For you personally, find the right leadership style to match the challenge of the business. A transformation will fail if you have a style that is not compatible with the business change you want to achieve.

While you must adapt to the environment requirements around you, your credibility and authenticity as a leader are key, so ask yourself which features of your character you want to amplify, and which you may need to dampen.

An audacious plan   04

Some people say 'Give the customer what they want', but that's not my approach. Our job is to figure out what they are going to want before they do.

STEVE JOBS, APPLE

In this chapter I will discuss the challenge of building a new vision, new objectives and a new plan for a company. I've used the story of 4G as the example. This was a technology that, in the UK at least, no-one really knew about. We saw an opportunity to show customers that they should expect more, that they could do more and that they should demand more from their mobile. We gave them something they never knew they needed – a pioneering technology that is now expected as standard.

Getting there wasn't easy, and this chapter provides some best practices on how to work with government and regulatory authorities to deliver a transformational plan.

The big bang theory

I officially began leading EE on 1 September 2011, almost two years to the day after the joint venture was created.

Over those two years, much work had been done to create the foundations of a significant British business. The original team, led by

Tom Alexander and Richard Moat, had managed to navigate the initial politics and regulatory hurdles of bringing two companies together. They had managed to steady the coming together of two ships and their crews that had been initially rocked by such a significant merger of equals. They had stabilized the new business and managed to ensure that the two brands of Orange and T-Mobile continued to perform in one of the most competitive markets in Europe.

The next stage was to move that business from a position of stability to a position of disruption and leadership within the industry. We tasked ourselves with doing something different. Something epic.

With my new team in place from day one, I took the helm of the company and we set about moving from stability towards a stampede of innovation. Ours was an ambitious and audacious plan, formed over a number of months with a number of different, but equally ambitious and audacious elements to it.

We were focused on creating a big bang both inside and outside of the company. Something that showed real difference through awesome action. We were looking to grasp the opportunity and create a deep transformation – not just within our business, but across the entire industry. And we were to do that by orchestrating a major event that would demonstrate our intentions.

In effect, we bundled together a set of big milestones which would be fused together on a single day to create maximum impact, galvanizing the organization, exciting our customers, stunning the industry and establishing a true leadership position. We were to take Orange and T-Mobile, two much-loved brands, and give them a new home, a new parent and a new super-powered sibling, seemingly overnight.

There were four key elements to our plan:

1 to introduce a new brand and business to the market;
2 to upgrade and integrate our retail estate under that brand;
3 to fully integrate our 3G and 2G mobile networks;
4 to launch a new 4G mobile network – the first in the UK, and two years ahead of the government's schedule – along with new devices that would be compatible from the start.

Coming up with the components of your big bang is relatively easy. Scoping them to ensure credible delivery is incredibly tough.

You need to ensure that every part of the organization is working in parallel, though often without the full picture due to reasons of company confidentiality. You also need to ensure that your systems don't fall over, that you can afford it, and that you can dedicate enough people to the cause while ensuring that business as usual does not suffer.

The outcome of all of this is that it is likely to cost your shareholders some serious money. If you need to transform a company quickly, your big bang needs to be really big and really loud.

Ours was just that – really big and really loud. It was a plan that sought to change the landscape of the British mobile industry with the creation of a new company, a new business, a new brand and a revolutionary new service.

It was also a secret. The best-kept secret in the industry in fact. To this day I still marvel at the fact that we managed to keep it quiet. The idea was so big, so dramatic and so challenging to our competitors that I was sure it was going to leak. But, despite needing to bring in many hundreds of people over many months, we managed to keep it under wraps.

We had our people sign legal non-disclosure agreements before participating. Most of those involved did not have the full picture and only received information about their relevant sub-project. These measures certainly helped to maintain confidentiality, but ultimately it was the culture in the team that made the difference. Everyone was excited to participate and knew that the project would have much less impact if the market knew about it beforehand.

The innovation vs regulation conundrum

Not only would launching a new network, new brand, and a new presence on the high street require the backing and belief of hundreds of employees, partners and suppliers, it would also require influencing the UK Government itself. For we were proposing to launch not only a new brand for Britain, but also a totally new communications standard – fourth-generation mobile spectrum, or 4G.

Essentially, mobile spectrum is an element of the radio frequency airwaves that mobile technology uses to transmit your voice, a video or bits and bytes of data from one place to another. 4G is essentially super-fast broadband on the move, meaning people could benefit from fixed-line fibre speeds without needing the fixed line – a network technology optimized for the mobile Internet on tablets and on smartphones.

Mobile spectrum is something that governments own – not businesses. A government generally leases these airwaves to a business. In this case, the UK Government's roadmap planned to allow mobile operators to bid for slices of this new 4G spectrum in just over two years' time (what would be 2014), and would allow the operators to implement the new services the year after that, in 2015.

I'm impatient at the best of times, but three years? Forget it. It made little sense for the people and businesses of Britain. In fact, the timetable only served the four big mobile operators Vodafone, O2, and our own – Orange and T-Mobile – who would be able to delay the launch of the next generation services and 'sweat' their existing 3G assets. It meant they could recoup more money from their 3G network investments, while their customers were paying for a service on a substandard, slower network. It would mean another three years of sluggish mobile Internet connections, poor e-mail download times, and patchy video calling.

The only people who would really be sweating were the customers. Britain prides itself on innovation and invention, but it had already fallen behind many other countries across the world, from those you would expect – such as the United States, South Korea and Japan – to others you might not, such as Azerbaijan and the Philippines.

This was a national embarrassment for the UK.

But of course, if you weren't aware this was the case – if no-one made the argument – you wouldn't really care. You wouldn't know what you *could* have and how much better your service *could* be unless someone told you. No-one was drawing up protest posters and marching on the House of Commons, screaming 'What do we want... 4G! When do we want it... now!'

Even if you did feel that passionately about mobile spectrum (and if you don't believe anyone could be, just ask my wife), governments are not known for bringing deadlines forwards. They don't take kindly to corporations diverting well-laid plans. We had to find a new way to launch 4G outside of the existing rules.

Doing the impossible

I distinctly remember the day we nailed it. It was a chilly October morning in Paddington, and we were having yet another meeting with the network team, challenging them on how to launch 4G without the required spectrum.

'It can't be done', had been the initial reaction. Quite fairly, some might say. We were, after all, dealing with the laws of physics, and without the spectrum we had no way of super-charging our 4G plans.

Network engineers are a funny bunch. I love them! They make magic happen, and on that day, one of them piped up from the corner and said, 'Why don't we try to use our existing network to launch 4G?'

The room fell silent and people turned to look at him. 'I mean, if we re-farmed our existing spectrum, we could still serve the customers that we have now, and also use a bit of it to launch the UK's first 4G network. Of course, the regulator will never allow it, but...'

We stopped him in mid-flow before he knocked down his own argument. He was right. It was possible. The joint venture had brought together the airwaves of two huge 1,800 MHz spectrum networks. By using a technique called 're-farming' we would be able to use a portion of that network to launch a version of 4G – a faster, super-powered mobile network – years before any other operator. While he hadn't quite bent the rules of physics, he *had* bent the rules within which we were thinking. In fact, with this new plan, there were no rules. This had never been done before. He was also spot on that the hurdle was a regulatory one. The competition would surely cry foul (they did), they would lobby against such a move (they did), and they would fight tooth and nail to try to stop it happening (they did). We in turn would have to argue for the right to launch a service that would benefit our business, as well as the businesses and people of Britain. We did. And we won.

But it wasn't easy. In fact, it was one of the most challenging aspects of my time as CEO of EE. The problem when dealing with big hairy regulatory issues such as this is that it will never entirely be in your own hands. This makes it by far the riskiest and hardest of situations to control and manage. However, it absolutely can be done.

As I have mentioned before in this book, these types of transform-ations are very hard on the leader of the organization because you have to always believe that it can be done, despite the lack of control. You have to drive it personally, because regulators and governments will not do what you want unless you engage with them directly. All the while, your competitors will use every trick in the legal book to slow you down or stop you.

In order to seek regulatory and government support, it is essential that you understand the personal and broader agendas of the govern-ment officials who call the shots. You have to understand how they operate, what's driving them, and how they make their decisions. This can only be done with strong and very experienced people in your organization. Ideally, they come with a senior background in the regu-latory or governmental arena. You cannot approach regulators and the government with an army full of business executives. Business people on their own in this environment are like Inuits in the Sahara. So, in the case of EE we hired an ex-regulator. Why? Because he had been on the other side of the fence and he knew who to speak to, about what, when and how. You also need a strong legal team but, in my experience, *never* lead with your lawyer. While the legal team will be absolutely essential in your understanding of the rules of the market environment, it is harder to build strong relationships with govern-ment and the regulatory authorities through a purely legal approach. So, use your legal team in the right way. At EE, they were invaluable in helping us understand the early potential negative actions from the competitors against our industrial plan. The competition will not shy away from using armies of lawyers to stop industrial policy – even when it is good for society and for the viability of the market. I'm of the firm belief that our competitors in the UK did their utmost to delay the introduction of 4G in the UK because they did not have an appetite to invest in the market at that time, their technology teams did not want to introduce 4G using their existing assets because it was against their plans, and they did not want us to succeed in driving net-work innovation before them. It became an intense regulatory, legal and PR battle that, in the end, we won. This would not have been possible without an exceptionally strong plan and the best legal, com-munications and regulatory teams in the industry.

If you have a similar battle to transform the regulatory and legal environment in your market, my advice would be to always lead with your government or regulatory expert – the person who can both deliver the business objectives and drive a broader picture.

The starting point is to articulate exactly what you need from the existing regulatory framework. Preferably, you need to give the expert team just one key objective. Regardless, they will still swamp you and the leadership team with risks, challenges, asks, and so on. Of course they will. That is part of their job. However, it is crucial to establish exactly what is absolutely required for the company to succeed. In our case, we needed to receive a change in our telecommunications licence. We needed to be allowed to use our existing airwaves for a new network technology – 4G.

Over the coming months, this became the single most important objective in the plans of the expert team and the legal function.

Working with governments and regulators

The next phase was to begin engagement with the necessary government and regulatory bodies. This was a huge education for me. I learned that, in order to be successful, at a minimum you will have to do the following things:

1 **Ask for something that is good not just for you, but for the country**
  If it is only good for your company, don't even start the conversation. You will not be successful. If you have something that is good for the country, you should consider investing in a broad external communications campaign about the issue to galvanize support. Of course, raising the issue in such a public way is also likely to give a platform to your competitors and their lobbying arms too.

2 **Drive the simplicity in your argument**
  If it is good for the country and good for your company, it is likely to be bad for someone else (probably your competitors or the shadow government). Therefore, it cannot just be compelling. It must also be totally clear and seemingly simple. If the proposition is good but complicated, it will be hard to gain broad support.

3 Know the style of government you're working with

If you are working with a government that is largely corrupt and does not have a true agenda for the society of the country, you might as well stop all your efforts in this area. You will be wasting your time. I have learned this the hard way in other markets. In these instances, you may wish to work with international bodies who can influence the country and with officials within the country who genuinely reform. Fortunately for us, this was not the case in the UK. No matter how much the British people moan about their politicians, this is a country with a generally fair and just system.

4 Be ready – and able – to compromise

If your project requires the regulator and government to do significant amounts of work and take a significant degree of risk, you need to be ready to trade on regulatory requests that may have an impact on your business, but are important to the regulator. This requires a lot of work up front with the team and probably with shareholders or your management to secure a negotiation framework and flexibility.

5 Build excellent relationships and find allies

Across the country there will be those who have similar requests or desires to yours. They can support you. Try to build a 'coalition' of supporters. I talked about 4G everywhere – all the time. Quickly, I started to find powerful individuals, companies, suppliers and technology gurus who were ready to go out there and fight on my side. At times it was amazing to see and feel that people were there, and helping to move the industry forward. We gained support early on – except of course from my competitors who hired the best lawyers they could find to fight us. They decided to compete with lawyers rather than with true innovation. Ultimately, they would fail.

6 Be open and transparent with government and the regulator

This is essential. Building a relationship with the right officials and driving trust through that relationship is a critical part of making this happen. Without trust and a mutual respect and understanding, you will not be successful.

7 Be bold and ready to take risks to defend your plan

During one of the many meetings with the regulatory authorities, I explained that I was going invest in the new 4G network technologies *before* they made their final decision. They could not believe that I would start a three-year investment programme at a cost of £1.5 billion without knowing if I could actually sell the service during 2012 and 2013. I simply said that my project made sense for the industry, for my 27 million customers, for employment, and for Britain. I had demonstrated that Britain was running behind the United States and other nations in rolling out this critical new telecommunications infrastructure. By investing already – before the final decision – I also showed the government they could reclaim industrial leadership in telecommunications from their European neighbours within 12 months if they supported the regulatory requests. It was a risk, but it worked.

8 Build in some extra time

Your timeline will most likely not match that of the government. The government and the regulator cannot execute like a business. They have to undertake legal due diligence at every turn – something that requires time and patience from every quarter.
And finally...

9 Make sure that it becomes YOUR plan

The leader of the business needs to be involved day in and day out in the delivery of this plan. You will have to promote and defend it personally. Nobody can replace you in talking to press, government, TV, employees, customers and lawyers in order to drive this to success at the finish line.

So, those were the big lessons I learned during the negotiations and altercations we had in our bid to get regulatory approval and launch the UK's first 4G network.

I also believe that I was lucky to be dealing with a regulator and government that were constructive, willing to listen, and who recognized the importance of a modern digital infrastructure for the country.

All in all, it was a complex, frustrating, nerve-wracking, but ultimately successful process.

It enabled us to move our ambition from being not just the biggest, but the best. A true British innovator. Our plan was forming, as was our vision.

Building a plan and a vision for the company

In previous roles, I had always held the firm belief that you have to have your vision and plan ready to go before you start the job. The argument goes that without the vision there is no context for the changes you need to make.

Interestingly, at EE we began building the vision for the company *after* we had restructured the management and established a leadership style. It worked fine. It actually allowed me to be even clearer, because I had been able to take more time to truly understand the opportunities and the risks. With our 4G regulatory plan now underway, we also had a clearer idea of our ambition and what we were setting out to achieve to support the creation of our new business. In the end, I announced the vision and the new plan when the business returned for the New Year in January 2012 – five months after I had started.

A vision is essential, but can be formed over time, often with the help and buy-in of your new team. Ultimately, the vision is incredibly important in gathering transformation momentum… once the line-up of your runners is on the track, the launch of your vision is the starting gun that really gets things moving.

There are some key rules to creating a vision for the business. First of all, a successful vision must be *your* vision, not the vision of whatever large and expensive consulting firm you might be using. Don't get me wrong, I have enormous respect for management consultancy firms. They can help in shaping and developing a vision. However, ultimately the vision must be yours.

Second, you must be personally excited about it. You have to feel passionate about it to deliver it well. You must be convinced that it can be done. You must stand behind it. You must also be able to communicate it in your own words. It doesn't matter if it is not perfect, but it has to be authentic.

Finally, your team must be aligned behind it. They have to be excited about it as well.

If you are in the process of redefining your company, you'd better do so with an ambitious, game-changing vision. There's no point squeezing out a marginally better purpose for your people and business than the one before. We are not looking for marginal gains here. We are looking for significant transformation. Make it big. Make it bold, but ensure it is credible and achievable. In my view, if a vision has no anchor in a few of the existing strengths of the company, it is practically impossible to achieve. Try to bring the core of your vision to the surface. Employees, customers, shareholders – everyone who you need to understand and engage with the vision – must recognize that, although ambitious, it is realistic and achievable. You need to strike that balance between it being real and revolutionary, credible and incredible.

The best transformative visions that I've been a party to or have developed myself always focus on how it will change the existing environment once you've achieved it. You have to be able to articulate the difference in customers' lives, in the market position, in the workplace and in the financial position. Ultimately, you need to ask, 'What will our future look like if we achieve this vision?' Even better, ask yourself, 'What will people miss if we do not exist in the future?'

Many companies make the mistake of starting with a financial aspiration. Revenue, cash flow, cost and profitability ratios are all a result of transforming to a new position. They are the fundamental financial metrics of a company, but they rarely build a purpose for a business. They are incredibly important, but they are results of transformation, action, and the execution of an important vision and plan.

The power of purpose

The key is to establish real *purpose* for your people through your vision and your plan. Purpose can establish true momentum, passion and motivation around transformation. The purpose is the reason beyond the paycheque why people come to work.

Steve Jobs was clear on Apple's purpose. He said that Apple would put a 'ding' in the universe.[14] That clearly worked!

EE is a smaller business with a different purpose. We decided to link our network vision to the UK itself. We believed that our plan was crucial for our customers, our company and our people – but most importantly for UK society and for future generations.

We saw that the UK's mobile infrastructure was totally out of kilter with the needs of its people. The United States, South Korea, Sweden and many other countries were ahead of the UK in the development of a new digital infrastructure, yet the UK uses the Internet more than other nations,[15] UK mobile subscriptions were growing at a faster rate compared to other nations[16] and UK workers commute more than their global neighbours.[17] So there was a rationale for establishing a real sense of urgency and purpose with our 15,000 employees as well as the thousands of employees working for subcontractors and suppliers to develop, build and market a better network.

Employees crave a purpose and every company has a key role to play in providing that purpose.

We were in the tricky position of being unable to reveal the specifics of what was to come – the launch of 4G, the birth of a new brand, the unveiling of a whole new business – but our manifesto was a reminder to our 15,000 employees of what we were here to do as a telecoms operator beyond the balance sheet – and what they were here to do beyond the paycheque. We were here to make sure that society could stay connected. That they could make calls to family hundreds of miles away. That they could send texts to friends just down the road. That they could work and play on the Internet from their phone, tablet, PC or TV. In its most basic form, we were saying loud and clear that, without a great network, you can't experience Apple's 'ding' – or any other company's ding for that matter. Without our network, smartphones were dumb and our societies would be disconnected from the wider world around them.

While I made it clear earlier that a vision cannot consist simply of a series of numbers, it is essential to link the vision and plan back to the financial result you are aiming for. The financial result that you agree upon needs to be pretty bullet proof and high-level enough so people can track back and map business success to it.

In our case, we committed to becoming the market leader in overall revenue, to improving our profitability to 25 per cent operational EBITDA, and to delivering double-digit cash flow growth. The plan had a three-year horizon.

Once you have defined your vision and the associated financial metrics, you need to communicate it across the entire company. That doesn't mean write and send an e-mail. You have to get out there. Your leadership team can support you on spreading the word, but if at all possible, the employees have to hear it from you before they hear it from anyone else. It has to be your story.

As I said earlier, it does not need to be perfectly polished. Authenticity is key.

I wrote the manifesto for the company during my Christmas break in 2011. My brand team were not happy. They kept saying that it was too technical and there was not enough excitement in it. They made a lot of changes. They even used our advertising agency to try to help – to polish it up. I looked at what this manifesto had become and, three days before I had to announce it, I changed everything back to my first version. I simply could not deliver the marketing version. I could not remember it, it didn't feel like mine, and my only option was to read it word-for-word from a piece of paper, verbatim, to the organization. Instead, I delivered my own version in my own Anglo-Dutch accent, using only a few scrawled notes written in my own (often illegible) handwriting. Admittedly a few bits were probably a little too technical for some, but the employees loved it. It was simple. It was credible. It worked.

If you're writing your plan and vision, my advice is to write it yourself and deliver it with energy and passion across all available internal communication channels. I used leadership meetings, all-employee WebEx calls, town hall meetings, coffee talks, e-mails, our intranet, video messages… everything I could. The job was to get people engaged with it, to get them trusting it, delivering it, living and breathing it.

Your plan and vision should be powerful enough that you do not need to update it frequently. Evolve it, but do not change path. I found updating it annually kept it real, credible and fresh.

It has to be big and bold, and you should use it as a framework through which you show the company's momentum. You should be able to give a progress report on it at your quarterly financial and major strategic announcements. It should form the DNA of your corporation upon which all else builds.

If you're considering developing a bold new plan it could be a game-changer for your business. It may redefine the industry and could set your company up for leadership and long-term differentiation. If your employees believe in it, it will boost morale and performance. It will certainly drive a reaction from your competitors.

Creating and relentlessly delivering on this new plan and vision is one of the most exciting parts of your company's transformation. It's challenging, it's difficult, but it will shape you and your company forever.

A step change in performance   05

A well-conceived strategy is important, but I could give our strategic plan to our competitors and not worry about it because it's all about execution.

DICK KOVACEVICH, WELLS FARGO

In this chapter we will discuss how to develop an environment inside your company where people have a bias for action and understand the discipline of getting things done. Most companies working in a specific industry will generally have the same business objectives and tools. I believe that if you can be better than the competition in execution, you will ultimately win. It is hard to instill a culture where employees focus on how they can use scarce resources efficiently and still deliver a better and timely output. If you have a real execution challenge, the starting point could be to appoint a Performance Officer. I had a brilliant one, who developed our model and whose work and ethos we shall learn about in this chapter.

Execution, execution, execution

So, we had a team. We had a vision. We had a plan. We had the beginning of something exciting.

But at the same time, we needed to take our performance to the next level. In 2011, we were in a period of relative stability. However, while the business was stable, the world around us was moving. That meant that stability – remaining as we were and just continuing to do what we were doing – would be dangerous. Doing so would mean being left for dust. We had to move along a different path if we were to maintain our leadership, and that meant significantly enhancing our performance – the performance of our people, the performance of our business, our financial performance... absolutely everything.

In the summer of 2011, I was reading a fascinating article in the *Harvard Business Review* about why businesses fail. In it, the authors stated, 'Most companies deliver only 60 per cent of their promised financial value. Why? Leaders press for better execution when they really need a sounder strategy. Or craft a new strategy when execution is the true weak spot.'[18]

For us, execution was our weak spot and we knew it. We were a big company born out of two huge businesses, and we were a mish-mash of both. There was no clear 'EE way' yet.

We needed to not just manage our performance, but to supercharge it. We needed a different level of execution, and we did that through a set of key tools that brought a rigidity and organization to the business that it hadn't seen before.

There are many companies that have failed because of strategic mistakes. Equally, companies that have a sound strategy very often do not deliver their full potential because of defects in their execution. I have observed many reasons for weak execution and underperformance during my career:

- Companies frequently reorganize with the objective of increasing their performance (eg from functional structures to integrated business unit structures, or the other way around). In such situations, accountabilities and responsibilities are often not clear enough from the top level down to the operating level.

- Companies have an abstract or unachievable vision about their business and for their employees (quite often developed by a brand agency who, in a bid to create an emotional response, don't ground that vision in reality).

- There isn't a strong enough management process based on a 'Balanced Scorecard' approach that translates the vision, strategy and priorities of the company into rigourously monitored financial and operational key performance indicators. We are referring to a 'balanced' model because it includes not just financial but also strategic non-financial measures. Most companies will have a financial Performance Dashboard but will not have a central repository of all other key indicators.

- Priorities are not made explicit and the incentives for managers and employees are not aligned well enough to the Balanced Scorecard metrics.

- Often, priorities are set well within one functional area or one business division but lack end-to-end alignment. In large organizations, it is essential to define what people are required to do for another team or function outside of their direct group.

- Businesses are very short-termist in their need to achieve 'the numbers', and have no clearly defined business plans based upon clear assumptions, priorities, plans and timetables.

- Managers and the organization are not focused enough on execution, delivering results or solving problems. For many it would seem that 'the details do not matter'.

- Projects are constantly delivered late and are often of poor quality without any consequence.

- There are a lot of initiatives – typically run by programme managers and often supported by consultants – that are often quietly closed without having achieved results, and then replaced by new initiatives.

- The management don't know their customers or their front-line teams well enough, and rely mainly on market research for guidance.

- Consultants are constantly present and are used for tasks that can and should be done internally. In the worst cases, expensive concepts frequently end up in a dusty drawer.

- There are frequent 'update meetings' to mainly discuss the 'what' with no clear agenda, preparation, decisions and follow-up. Quite often this comes along with a 'powerpoint culture', when people try to create beautiful business artwork instead of spending their time coming up with sharp analysis, options, proposals or solutions.

The Performance Management Framework

Ultimately, a performance management system should be developed through a set of goals and key performance indicators (KPIs) that are interwoven – and often shared – by departments and individuals throughout the organization. To get it right is harder than it sounds – especially in complex businesses.

The Performance Management Framework that we implemented at EE proved to be an effective instrument in creating a high-performance organization.

Who was the master behind this? I explained earlier that I decided to install a chief performance officer. He developed and executed the concept brilliantly. Guess which country he's from? Germany, of course. Stereotype or not, it is officially the land where efficiency is at the heart of the nation's success (and I say this as a Dutchman).

An effective performance management system is typically based on the following process steps, which cover the 'what' and 'how' of achieving ambitious goals in the business.

You set the direction and context through strategic and market planning, then execute and manage operational and commercial performance through five drivers:

1 Establish clear metrics, targets and accountability.

2 Create realistic budgets and plans.

3 Track performance effectively.

4 Hold robust performance conversations.

5 Ensure rewards, consequences and actions.

The outcome of this process is that you can measure real value for your business, for yourselves and for your shareholders.

Figure 5.1 The EE Performance Management Framework

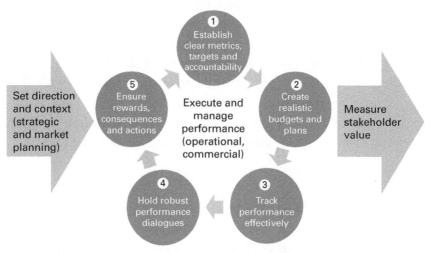

SOURCE Ralf Brandmeier

Aligning performance to the vision

The performance system needs to be based on a focused and tangible vision that has to clearly express the value proposition of the company. At EE, our simple vision was:

> To deliver the best network and the best service so that our customers trust us with their digital lives.

This is what we believed we needed to do in order to differentiate ourselves in the market. Our belief was that if we focused on this vision and rigorously measured it, ensuring everything we did hooked back into its key constituent parts – the best network, the best service and the drivers of trust for people's lives in the digital age – then it would drive our success.

The definition of priorities, our planning and communication activities, and our measurements all centred around this vision – and EE's employees continue working towards it to this day.

The expression of the vision needs to be short, clear and simple. It cannot only be aspirational. It needs to be achievable and based on the key assets and potential strengths of the company.

The performance system must define over-arching key indicators that measure the success of the company in implementing its vision.

In our case, we had clear technical network indicators, such as mobile network coverage across the country and the number of 'dropped calls' per customer (ie the number that failed to connect or lost connection during the call itself). We measured the best service through Net Promoter Scores (see Chapter 8 for more details).

Being critical, we could not operationalize 'trust us with their digital lives' properly using pure market share targets to analyse our success and failure rates in this area. As a result, I often struggled with this element of our vision. Crystal-clear measurement is key.

Setting the direction

The process starts with the formulation of clear statements relating to the strategic direction of the business – the 'what'.

At EE we updated our strategic priorities every year to reflect our response to market opportunities and challenges. These statements were typically defining priorities for our business such as:

- Extending and leveraging our network leadership to drive profitable growth (to be delivered through ambitious network and commercial roadmaps).

- Realizing a market-leading cost base (to be achieved by capturing planned synergies and effective cost efficiency programmes across the organization).

- Becoming the service leader in the market (to be realized by robust processes and systems and a high quality of products and services).

- Growing our market share in specific areas of opportunity or historic under-performance (in the business market by focusing on success with large corporate business-to-business customers or the public sector, and in the consumer market by extending our reach beyond pure mobile phones and into tablet computers).

- Driving important enablers (such as creating a great place to work for our employees, or IT stability).

These priorities are the basis for the definition of specific objectives, measures, targets, initiatives and budgets that guide actions and align the organization for effective strategy execution.

Instilling clear accountabilities and responsibilities

Having clear accountabilities and responsibilities in an organization is essential for an effective execution of the strategy and its underlying plans. It is advisable to put the necessary effort into this after – or in parallel with – a reorganization, especially when companies operate within matrix organizations. A simple tool we used was a matrix focusing on the accountabilities and responsibilities of the functions to achieve the strategic priorities and the financial and operational objectives. We forced a clear definition of which functional area was accountable for a key strategic priority and which areas were responsible for the delivery of programmes or people supporting the same priority.

For example, we had a functional consumer marketing management area which was accountable for the delivery of profit and loss of this business. The sales organization, meanwhile, had key responsibilities to ensure the successful delivery of the consumer business revenue targets.

Typically, when assessing accountabilities and responsibilities, the following need clarification:

- Interfaces between finance and business units owning marketing or a specific profit and loss segment.
- Interfaces between sales channels and business units.
- Interfaces between business functions and support areas such as Human Resources, Strategy, Finance and Legal.

As a first step, implementing this requires clarification and agreement within the top team, which will in turn require much debate and discussion. On

(Continued)

paper everything seems clear, but in practice people will have different understandings about the various accountabilities and responsibilities. This gets especially tricky – and is essential to get right – when agreeing where the responsibilities and accountabilities begin and end between specific individuals or departments across the different functions.

Getting your team to commit

Alongside the creation of these performance tools we also created a series of CEO and chief **commitment memos** – the top team's detailed commitments to the business. In a structured way, each of my direct reports would outline how their organization contributes to the overall strategic priorities of the company. We started with a series of shared company goals that were used to identify the specific part each department plays. Each document was explained and reviewed by the whole leadership team. Each individual commitment memo described in detail the goals, objectives, available resources, structure, required support from other teams, key inputs into other teams, and specific processes.

Here's an example of the content structure we used at EE for the chief's commitment memos:

- **State of the business**: a transparent view of the achievements from the previous year and the areas identified as needing improvement.

- **Commitments**: the details of the functional priorities and commitments. These could be commercial ambitions, critical projects, transformation initiatives or organization development plans.

- **Plans and delivery milestones**: these specified how and when the function would deliver its commitments with precise activities and timings.

- **A Balanced Scorecard**: these consisted of the relevant company objectives, KPIs and targets to measure performance based on the classic perspectives of the company financials, customer satisfaction and loyalty scores, internal processes, and employee satisfaction and productivity.

Once completed, this can then be cascaded throughout the organization and to every individual within every nook and cranny of the business. Doing so not only sets the expectations of a leader, it clarifies the role that an employee plays in delivering key elements of the business strategy. It shows how that individual plays their part in delivering on the bigger picture. It also demonstrates that the company is ready and clear about what the organization needs to accomplish and how it intends to do it. At EE we provided a full version of the chief's commitment memos to the first line of management, while all other employees would receive a summary that excluded sensitive information.

Once employees understand the strategy and plans, the next important part of the process is to reinforce their execution by setting personal objectives that have a clear line of sight to those plans. Incentives and bonuses need to be linked to the attainment of employee, business unit *and* corporate objectives.

Once you have developed the complete Performance Management Framework and the HR department has developed a good incentive mechanism for every employee (covering personal, functional and corporate objectives), you can start focusing on monitoring performance and, importantly, the impact you're having on your customers.

The power of the Performance Dashboard

Experienced managers know that 'what you measure is what you get' and that strong management systems affect the behaviour of both managers and employees.

The company Performance Dashboard is a tool that monitors the company KPIs and their alignment to the commitments that have been made. It complements the financial measures with operational measures that are the drivers of future performance. An example of this would be customer satisfaction, internal processes, and the organization's innovation and improvement activities.

Typical KPIs can be the status of important projects, IT stability, customer satisfaction across all customer touchpoints, customer service levels, status of transformation initiatives, employee satisfaction, brand awareness, development of new business areas, the commercial performance across all sales channels, financial delivery and headcount.

The dashboard should be reviewed every month in the executive board, including highlights and lowlights, followed by decisions on corrective actions. It should also be shared with the wider management community to provide true transparency about the situation your business is in.

The importance of getting to know the customer and the front line

Alfred P Sloan was CEO, President and Chairman of General Motors from the 1920s through to the 1950s. He turned it into one of the world's leading companies and is quoted as saying:

> It may surprise you to know that I have personally visited, with many of my associates, practically every city in the United States, from the Atlantic to the Pacific and from Canada to Mexico. On these trips I visit between five and ten dealers a day. I meet them in their own places of business, talk with them across their own desks and solicit from them suggestions and criticisms as to their relations with the corporation.

There is no better example of the importance of a leader being close to the front line.

Front-line teams – whether in retail or service, be they direct employees or franchised dealers – are the lifeblood of your company. They are the living embodiment of your brand. And they know your customers better than anyone else in the company.

Spending time with them allows you to identify new opportunities, from more innovative products and services to better cost and process efficiencies – right through to new ways to improve customer satisfaction. In the context of performance management, this is the moment where you can link your KPIs with reality. Producing dashboards and measuring KPIs alone is not sufficient to successfully manage a business. Being at the front line, talking to sales and service people and listening to customers allows you to truly understand what's going on behind the measures, the metrics and the numbers. It also ensures you are working on the right priorities and that the rest of the company is effectively supporting the front line to be successful.

At EE we institutionalized the philosophy of spending time with – and learning from – our front-line teams:

- Our top management frequently visited shops and call centres to find out what the company could do better in order to support the agents to better serve our customers. After every visit we produced a list of actions, which was then followed up in a disciplined way by all relevant functions.

- All senior managers would also visit our shops and call centres on a regular basis. Agents and operations managers would feel respected when they saw that their feedback and input had been listened to and acted upon.

- Later on we even started to develop a more formal approach, whereby managers from HQ would be assigned to a specific store and establish even more interaction.

- Every Monday morning we would share the previous week's findings, reviewing customer satisfaction results, key events and drivers such as complaints and IT stability. We would then discuss how to execute functional plans to improve service levels, process efficiencies and customer satisfaction.

Here leadership by example is very important. I visited scores of our stores every year and at least one of our call centres every month, learning directly from our store and service agents. I would also take the opportunity to talk with our customers and meet with the store and operation managers to understand first-hand what was working well and what needed to improve. This massively boosted the morale of our employees and set high expectations for our managers. It was also a lot of fun, and kept me real as a leader.

I remember visiting one of our top London stores. I had been there a number of times before and the manager Lisa recognized me immediately. As with most of our central London stores, it was very busy on the floor, so Lisa asked if I wouldn't mind helping out with a customer. He had an issue with his phone settings. I managed to solve the issue, and afterwards, Lisa and I found a few quiet minutes in which to talk about the good and the bad. I felt proud that day, because I was not treated like the king on the hill. She treated me like a colleague. I was also proud that I could help directly and learn from customer issues. This was the culture I wanted.

Often the science of performance management can leave people cold. Some people see it as a dry subject. However, I cannot stress just how essential it is. It's the framework on which the success of your company will be built. With the right tools in place you have a code-breaking machine that allows you to make sense of the levers at your disposal to counteract the inefficiencies within your business. It will enhance your company and your people's performance. It will help you strike gold.

I've no doubt that that your company has a defined set of solid financial goals and objectives. It probably has a very clear overview of accountabilities for the individual organizations, and an incentive system to support these. However, it's worth challenging yourself to ensure the non-financial strategic objectives that have been set are monitored with the same rigour as the financial ones. Are you sure that the individual business areas understand what they have to deliver themselves and as a set of cross-functional departments? Are they incentivized to support the strategic priorities of a different functional area, and do all strategic objectives ladder up to the ultimate vision of your organization?

A Performance Management Framework can help to execute better, and execution is key to the success of every business.

Building a new brand for Britain 06

It is almost impossible to be an exceptional organization or enjoy exceptional success by doing what everyone else is doing. However, a lot of companies lack the courage and fear being different because of pressure from competitors, boards, senior management, and shareholders, who seek positive quarterly sequential results. Doing what we've always done seems safer.

CHARLES O'REILLY, GRADUATE SCHOOL OF BUSINESS, STANFORD UNIVERSITY

Changing a brand or introducing a new brand can be an expensive and risky adventure. This chapter will share with you how we did it successfully. I'm hoping this may help you avoid some of the key mistakes in developing your own brand identity, promise, look and feel, or execution.

As mentioned earlier in the book, this is a unique case study. There are not many business books that lead you down the path of creating a completely new brand from two well-known, much-loved and successful brands already operating in the market. However, that's exactly what we did, and in this chapter you'll find out why.

Trust me, there was method behind this madness!

The secret project

Throughout the last few chapters I've been referring to our company as EE. I've done that to ensure ease of understanding by the reader.

However, by rights, I shouldn't be referring to the company in that way at all, because in our narrative, EE hasn't actually been revealed as a company or a brand yet.

We're still nine months away from that. It's Christmas 2011, and the business is in quite a different place to where it is today.

We're running a company called Everything Everywhere that is essentially the corporate entity of our two brands, Orange and T-Mobile. Both our brands serve UK consumers and businesses with Pay Monthly and Pay as you Go mobile services. Orange also has a fixed-line broadband company that is starting to turn around after a long time in the doldrums.

As part of the transformation of our business, we had already kicked off 10 projects that were designed to create a new leader in the mobile market. The 10 were made up of front-of-house 'big bang' projects, as well as some more unsung, unseen yet critical back-end support elements that would support the more public aspects of our launch.

Hundreds of people across the business were working on these 10 transformation projects, and while they were working on their own element of the plan, they also knew a little about each of the others – at least the project title, aspiration and objective. That was important to ensure that project interdependencies matched up and worked well. All 10 of these projects were generally about bringing the infrastructures of Orange and T-Mobile together (the mobile networks, the retail estates, the systems and so on) to form a backbone for the business from which the two brands would operate. This was being done to drive efficiencies within the joint venture – both financial and procedural.

But there was another project – a secret project that none of the transformation teams were aware of. The re-branding of the business. The creation of EE.

This was a particularly challenging project, not least because we had 27 million customers and 15,000 employees who had wedded themselves to a particular brand for a reason. On the part of our customers, they voted for Orange and T-Mobile with their wallets on a monthly basis. For our employees, they had applied for jobs at the company of their choice because something about it spoke to them personally.

We were now on a path where we would ultimately ask these two massive and passionate communities to leave history and emotion behind and believe in something new.

It would require our plans to be driven to inch-perfect precision – and we would also need a little bit of luck.

These opportunities are very rare in one's career. It was an opportunity to redefine who we were and what we could do. It was the opportunity for us to break out of the historic belief that we were an industry focused on voice, text and a little bit of web on the move, and redefine what the mobile device and mobile networks are all about – connectivity.

We built the company's DNA around that idea – about how technology can make people's lives better.

It was to be a digital brand for a digital age, and it began with a rallying cry to a select few within the business. We said: 'In September 2012, we will launch an all new, market-leading, game-changing brand.'

A brand is so much more than a logo or a tag line. It's a promise. It's the very essence of your company and forms the basis of an emotional contract between you and your customers. The building blocks of your brand can create an often intangible connection with them, but will also form part of the rational consideration they make during a first-time or repeat purchase. Your brand brings together all of the constituent parts and reasons why they chose you over the competition. Your brand embodies your business – what you stand for, what you believe and what you promise to your customers.

Brand transformation

Brand transformation is one of the hardest projects in a company. The key challenge is finding people with experience in this area. The fact is, because it is a unique and rare career opportunity, you are unlikely to find people in your organization who have done this before.

A brand transformation can bring enormous additional value. It can give you access to new product markets and new customer segments. It can help you reduce marketing costs by leveraging brand awareness and consideration. It can strengthen employee engagement.

It is also very costly and can carry significant risk. Customers may not like the new brand. Employees may not endorse it. It is especially risky if the existing brands you are dealing with are well known, international, and successful.

It is not something you do lightly. You have to have very good reasons to decide to undertake a brand transformation.

At EE, we decided to introduce a new brand for several reasons.

While awareness for our existing brands Orange and T-Mobile were strong – especially Orange, which had over 80 per cent spontaneous awareness – they were developed in a different time and for a different age.

In the UK, our brands were very much rooted in a world where you used your phone to make voice calls rather than for accessing YouTube or Facebook. We had two options – to either reinvigorate our existing brands and focus them on the new digital generation, or introduce a new one.

Orange had built incredible brand strength in the consumer market but lacked traction in big business and in adjacent product categories like the fixed-line business.

T-Mobile had built up a reputation as a real challenger in Pay as you Go and for ethnic and small business communities, but was struggling to gain traction as a real player in the digital age. It was very strong in London, but less powerful outside.

We needed a brand that would give us permission to win in these areas – and create new pockets of leadership that resonated with a more digital Britain.

We had also identified a mismatch between our vision of focusing on network differentiation, and the existing brand identities. Neither of our existing brands were perceived as great network innovators. This was a position owned by Vodafone due to their grounding as a technology-centric company and the fact that they had a strong history as one of the nation's incumbent mobile operators. It is extremely hard to change the customer perception of an existing brand. It is especially hard if that perception is totally the opposite of what you want it to be. In my view, if you need a complete repositioning of your propositions and differentiation, it is better to start afresh, despite the risks. And that's what we did.

Rationale for a new brand

We also had other considerations. I wanted to create a fresh, new, modern company culture. We had to move away from the two separate cultures built up over many years, and toward a single, powerful one. Of course, there were many positive elements in the existing cultures, but some of the cultural traits – many of which had grown organically over time – created an environment that was not set up to succeed. We had to get rid of some of the bad attributes such as slow execution, no real focus on the front line, and a lack of understanding and interest in technological innovation. At Orange, for example, many of the technology and service teams felt isolated and under-appreciated. But, while Orange was a strong consumer brand with positivity and a promise of a bright future, what was the company if not a technology and service business? To this day, I think some people believed we were in the cinema tickets industry! It was proof of a successful marketing campaign perhaps,[19] but the absence of any real focus on the fundamentals of network and service was a danger to the heart and soul of the business. I felt the need to re-boot our people's understanding of the core values and fundamentals of our new business. And to do that, we needed to do something significant, new and magnificent.

As we analysed the DNA of the existing brands it became clear that they did not embody some of the fundamental elements that we needed to successfully execute our company transformation. The Orange brand had very strong attributes around trust, friendliness and warmth, but we needed to attract customers who were more biased towards innovation, technology, speed and industrial dynamism.

It is very hard to describe your brand DNA – especially if you are a third- or fourth-generation employee, but it is important to try your best to distill and understand it.

The way customers unconsciously perceive your brand is absolutely crucial to your understanding of how to sell and market something different – and how to take your business to a different place.

All this being said, you must not take the redefinition or creation of a new brand lightly. Whatever's right for your business, if you are looking at augmenting elements of your brand – or inventing a new one – it is a major undertaking and carries with it huge amounts of risk.

For us, another key hurdle in the creation of a new brand was our company name, which we wanted to link to the customer and employee brand. Behind the scenes, our name was Everything Everywhere, which already had negative internal and external baggage. Employees found it difficult and the media were having a field day mocking it.

Created as a name to unify two disparate teams around a single, simple idea, it was revealed in 2010.

Initially, it was meant to sit in the background – predominantly as an internal name only – with a logo that was designed with a light grey tone to make sure that our two existing brands remained the heroes of the business – a blast of orange, a splash of magenta, bursting out of the neutral greyness of the Everything Everywhere palette.

But it quickly became an irritant for many in the business, its bombastic nature naturally coming to the fore, driving conversation and consternation.

Containing a tongue-twisting 20 letters, it was a name that stopped people in their tracks – sometimes for the right reasons, sometimes for the wrong. Either way, for our 10,000 sales and service people it was a real pain. It caused them unnecessary extra work when writing the name down or explaining what it meant to our customers. It was not practical. Plus, the name, which was representative of a bigger, better, stronger telecommunications network from which you can access 'everything' you want 'everywhere' you go, was launched when the network was not performing well enough to make that claim.

So, it was time for change.

The core of a new brand

Firstly we began two months of investigation, including qualitative and quantitative research, considering different brand options including the launch of a new one.

The key to this work was to uncover which segments of the market we could not address with our existing brands. In our case, we discovered that over half of British consumers simply would not consider Orange or T-Mobile when buying a new mobile contract. We also analysed brand case studies (both good and bad) from industries outside our own. We looked at DHL and Deutsche Post, who had done a pretty good job of re-branding in Germany. In particular, they had done well in gaining employee support and understanding for the change. We also investigated Santander and Abbey from the UK market. What we learned quickly was that every re-branding exercise was different. It was difficult to find a precedent for our plan.

After months of preliminary work, the research showed us unequivocally that it would take significant time and money to properly rejuvenate and reposition our existing brands. If we continued with just the two brands we had, their legacies would slow our success down. It showed us that the opportunities open to us if we were successful in introducing a new brand were so great, that it was worth accepting the risks.

But it was still a hard decision. Most people, wedded by years of history, stories and passion for the two existing brands, believed we simply needed to refresh what we already had. The facts and figures from the research told a different story.

They told us that ours was a commoditized market with declining spend on telephony. We found that mobile networks weren't considered to be a part of the future in the same way that Facebook, Skype or Apple were. Ours was a passive and transactional relationship with customers. We wanted to change that.

A new brand would give us permission to do something we hadn't done before. It was a rare, once-in-a-generation opportunity to do something special – create a brand that would impact everyone in the UK.

There were some clear statements that we believed in as we worked through this:

1 The role technology plays in our lives has never been greater.

2 New technologies create new possibilities.

3 Brands win not on what they say but on what we can do with them.

But we were also acutely aware that people thought that technology was a frustration – not an enabler. That technology took too long to work, that it cost too much, or was just difficult to use. And our industry – the networks – had often been a part of that problem.

But the opportunity was there. Mobility, we knew, was becoming fundamental and the UK was on the cusp of a technology boom. Already the country had the highest penetration of smartphones, digital TVs, Internet TVs and e-commerce users in Europe. It also had the highest usage of mobile Internet and social networking, and of Internet per month in the home.

The added fact that we already had 27 million customers, 15,000 staff and over 700 stores, meant we had a potent mix – a real opportunity to do something different.

We concocted a plan to show everyone in the UK how the magic of technology can make the everyday better – to create a network that would make your whole digital life easier.

And with it, we created a single, powerful underlying brand promise that would give us focus and guide us in everything from the creation of propositions to the development of our advertising: *If you ever thought you couldn't do this or couldn't do that… Now You Can.*

Brands typically *tell*. Ours would *show*.

Estimating the costs of such an exercise is hard. We built our business case on a number of assumptions, including:

- the requirement for an additional 2 per cent of revenue to launch the new brand over a six-month period (on top of our existing product and demand generation spend);

- a significant above-the-line budget;

- a dedicated budget for below-the-line communication that would support in explaining the new brand to existing customers;

- capital expenditure (CAPEX) costs to change and create our websites, retail estate and buildings;

- IT costs (mainly calculated separately as part of each individual transformation programme);

- training costs and brand engagement activities for employees.

That last point was absolutely key. We needed to get our employees believing, selling and telling people about our new brand. It is hugely important to dedicate funds to indoctrinate your entire company into the new brand. A new brand will fail if it is not carried by your employees.

The creation of a new brand

So, in front of you is a blank canvas. How do you build a new brand? Firstly, if you do not have experience in-house, hire specialized firms who do this for a living. This is one of the rare areas where I have used external specialized consultants. Personally, I'd recommend you do not use general management consultancy firms who have some experts in this area. Instead, go straight to the companies who *only* do this type of work. You also need to have an internal team dedicated to working on it. I spent a significant amount of my time working on this element of our plan.

The starting point is to write a brand narrative, which we split into three parts – our ambition, our ability to achieve that ambition, and how we act and behave.

This wasn't a fancy presentation, a film or even storyboards. It was just one A4 page – but it was essential in kick-starting creative scenarios.

Only about 20 people out of 15,000 in the business were involved at this stage, and we tried hard to build consensus between us wherever possible. That's a hard thing to do because words, pictures and creative ideas all mean different things to different people. There are unspoken nuances at every turn. One man's green is another man's blue. One woman's digital revolution is another woman's digital disillusion.

After three months of work, in the run-up to Christmas 2011, we had a brand narrative and ambition that we had agreed upon – the *Now You Can* plan.

However, all was not well in the camp. We were still working with the name Everything Everywhere, and after eight weeks of work on the look and feel, we had ended up with a series of interconnected bubbles, a few purple-coloured blobs and a brand architecture that had created total crisis within the team.

These were tough times. Creative folk are often high in emotion, and we had all succumbed to being creative folk during these last three months.

Furious debate and passionate discussion were the norm. I would not have wanted it any other way. This was, after all, the DNA of our business that we were trying to create.

The key decisions were always taken with my entire leadership team in the room. You want to make sure that people can express their horror, pleasure and full range of emotions throughout this process, as this whole exercise can be quite a subjective and personal one.

We spent many hours locked in a big meeting room, looking at a number of different creative scenarios. Each scenario was developed around the central Now You Can premise, but was built to demonstrate how the key underlying building blocks of a potential above-the-line campaign could work – how the colour palette, the font, the picture style, the tone of voice, the key language tone would look, feel and sound.

My brand team and their leader were really smart. They did an excellent job. They guided the team to the right answer by demonstrating a large number of scenarios that we ultimately rejected. We started to understand what would and would not work. Following our initial months of crisis, they drove consensus around the direction of the brand architecture. They were able to build a number of analogies with existing brands and their respective fonts, colours, tones of voice, language and visuals. This helped us to understand the overall concept of a brand architecture and started to highlight how a brand architecture is essential in building a long-term sustainable brand. We looked at what lay within strong, powerful brands. We looked at BMW, *The Sunday Times*, Virgin, Google. We looked at strong brands, and started to play with their key underlying building blocks. It was incredibly engaging and enlightening, but it was very hard to take the right decisions.

We ended up with a framework that focused on a dynamic brand with a dynamic design and a unique flexible colour palette ranging from aqua to yellow to grey. We did not want to be stuck with a static palette or design because modern brands – such as Google – are able and confident enough to present themselves differently at different times. We also needed to use unique colours that were not associated with the major operators. Vodafone is red, O2 is blue, T-Mobile is magenta and Orange is, well, Orange.

Our language was going to be short, clear and with a sense of humour. I believe that humour is key – especially when you bring a new brand into a mature market, where companies have over-promised and consumers are both knowledgeable and sceptical about mobile telecommunications. So, ours would be a brand that was purposeful and focused on the useful things that matter every day. But it was also playful – we would never take ourselves too seriously.

We also decided to try to be local from the start, to represent all of our millions of customers right across the country. We planned to deploy regional marketing communications, public relations and events, championing the local towns and cities where we would launch 4G first.

As a mobile operator, one of the hardest parts of communicating with your customers is knowing how to visually articulate airwaves, spectrum, an invisible network. We wanted to crack that, and bring our core product – our network – to life in advertising for the first time. So the font and typography we picked were unique and used 'particles' to form words and letters. The particles represented our network and allowed us to visualize messages better.

EE was designed as a digital brand for the digital age – fun, meaningful, modern and fresh, with a tone of voice that matched. When we launched our superfast network, we did so with the OM4G campaign. When we landed in Scotland, our billboards screamed Glasgooooo! And when we pushed in business – for this was a brand built for enterprise as well as consumers – we did so with the play on words, 'Boardvroom'.

New brand guidelines

So, our brand DNA was coming together. We now had a fully-fledged brand ambition, architecture, and accompanying assets – words, pictures, particles. But it's one thing having pictures on pages and boards – it's another thing to actually implement them in a consistent and meaningful way. This is why you need a clear set of branding guidelines. They enable a consistency in advertising, messaging, and communications. It's a fairly technical piece of work. It is extremely hard to secure execution across all the communications channels and routes to market consistent with the final guidelines. We organized frequent 'immersion' sessions to review and critique the outcome of the guidelines. We built mock retail stores, reviewed website layout across the walls of large meeting rooms with blacked-out windows.

We read messaging scripts for products, reviewed proposed customer letters, pawed over mock-up customer text messages and e-mails – all within the confines of the new brand guidelines. It required an incredible amount of work. One of the biggest difficulties for us was to get the retail store right and in line with the guidelines. Building a mock shop with the right affordable furniture and set-up that's in line with these rules was the hardest piece of the puzzle. The first time we built a mock store, it looked like a kindergarten from Ikea. It was way too busy, there were too many colours and it was cluttered with demo equipment. It looked absolutely bizarre, but, according to the rulebook, was completely in line with our branding principles! The challenge with a dynamic physical space such as a store is that it's possible to implement very different versions of the truth.

Again, it was very important to visit these test areas with the entire leadership team and the people who were responsible for building the end products in line with the brand. The team grew closer throughout this arduous but exciting process, and together each individual uncovered new areas where we needed to improve. As we lived and worked with it, we also started to understand and engage with the brand more and more. The cynics in the team started to warm up and we quickly ended up as a band of business risk takers who were willing to put their reputations on the line and launch a new brand for Britain.

By the spring of 2012, after many months of back and forth, tears and tantrums, we were now firmly on a journey to becoming a one-brand company. One brand for all our customers – whether that be consumer, business, mobile or fixed line – and one brand for all our employees.

Maintaining the existing brands

We were clear that we wanted to keep our Orange and T-Mobile customers stable and happy and take them on the EE journey with us. We wanted to make sure that getting to EE as the single brand – the ultimate end game – went without a glitch, easing the pressure on all the operational issues going on behind the scenes to make this final step happen. We wanted to give EE the time to grow, developing the right propositions for the new brand, not launching an old set of propositions with a new name. And we wanted to reduce the financial risk of trading only with EE in the super-competitive UK marketplace – by moving and attracting customers to it gradually.

To do this, we needed to maintain our existing brands and to launch EE into the market as both a parent and a peer brand. EE ran the house, but it was also to be the sibling to its two older brothers. It was, at first glance, a strange family, but we identified clear roles, belief systems and positioning for each of our brands. Each had a reason for being.

EE would be the new network for your digital life. We would focus strategically on getting entirely new customers onto EE. So, as well as moving existing people over to the new brand, we aimed to attract a whole new set of customers to join the EE family. During this time, we'd need to invest in building awareness and understanding of the EE brand. We would do that not just by telling, but by doing. We would invest and launch in new propositions that would make EE the first choice. We would have a broad range of propositions beyond mobile, propositions for all of your digital life. It meant broadening our horizons in terms of the types of offers we provided, as well as broadening the way we were set up. Our people would be the driving force behind all of this. We invested in them to make them the specialists – experts in not only operating systems, but also experts at making all of these technologies and services easy for people to understand and use.

For **Orange** and **T-Mobile** customers, it would be evolution, not revolution. We planned to offer existing customers the chance to migrate to EE. They'd get a better deal if they did. However, if upgrading to EE was not for them, or it simply wasn't the right time to make a change, we'd make sure they stuck with us. And we planned to continue to acquire new Orange and T-Mobile customers, allowing those people who wanted to be on those brands to join those brands.

Product innovation at the core of your brand

It is absolutely essential that your new brand launches in parallel with a major new product range. If you don't do that, all you have is a sparkly new font and some freshly painted shops. A brand is a promise, and that promise needs to be backed up with action. Today's educated modern consumer requires, more than ever before, a closer link between that brand promise and the product they receive. There is no point launching a new brand without a clear, new and innovative breakthrough proposition. Preferably, you will have a whole range of new products, services, and solutions. Today's leading new digital brands, such as Google and Facebook, launched with totally unique products and services.

For EE, behind the launch of this exciting and vibrant brand lay true innovation – the thing that our promise was built upon... the 4G network. Along with it would come new devices, new tariffs, new services. But at its heart was this new superfast mobile technology.

To deliver this was as challenging as designing the brand itself.

In order to transform a product portfolio, you need to have excellent engineers, smart strategic thinkers and dedicated product marketing people. Most companies have these but lack common goals, alignment, and integration in these areas. They tend to live in silos.

In our case it was worse. The technology department was treated like a cost centre. Brand, marketing, pricing, and sales were seen as sexy. Networks and IT were the geeks no one seemed to speak to or care about. They were seen as areas of the past – not the future – with employees (predominantly male) who had been with the company longer than in any other department. Nobody understood what they were doing, let alone what they could develop for the future. This isolation and excommunication of our technical team had created an environment of disillusion. If you wanted something done, the answer was mostly 'No – we have no budget and no time for that'. Our marketing team knew more about loyalty points, pricing, and applications than about our own key product, the telecommunications network.

I took on the task of putting technology and innovation back at the heart of our organization, and turning the geeks into the heroes of our business. The first step in re-establishing a focus on innovation is to focus your attention on it as the leader. I did this to the point of obsession.

During the first week in my job, I asked to review the network's key performance indicators versus our benchmarks. It was remarkable. We were green across the board when compared to our direct competitors, but the benchmarks we used were red against our international competitors. The technical team tapped me on the shoulder and told me not to worry. The benchmarks were in line with the UK competition. I started immediately re-setting the targets. I made it clear that if we wanted to be the best, we had to work to international standards, not the poor levels of our competitors. We had to establish a new benchmark. I installed a live screen in my office from which I could personally monitor the real-time performance of our network across our country. During every meeting with Marketing, Sales, Finance – in fact during every meeting – I would talk about our network. The organization went through a steep learning curve. I demonstrated little or no patience for people in critical communications roles who did not include the network – our core product – in their messaging and campaigns.

Finally, the business started to listen. This much-needed spotlight on technology helped to establish a discussion around innovation and transformation. It was ultimately the psychological shift that helped the business get behind the launch of 4G.

This kind of change will require more time and energy than you think. It can take months and sometimes years to ensure the complete focus of the organization. But focus, determination and obsession on the critical topics are essential.

Going back to the core

In order to start innovating, you have to clarify what your existing product range really is – where it is good and bad, how it stacks up against the competition and how it compares to similar products in other countries. It sounds very basic, but most companies tend to forget where they can and should innovate. A lot of companies start looking outside at innovation and try to project those ideas on their own business. In the world of telecommunications operators, everyone dreams of developing new 'over-the-top' applications and services rather than innovating on their core networks. Maybe that's because these over-the-top applications look and sound sexier than the inner workings of the nodes in a network. But it was due to this lack of appetite to invest in network CAPEX – this disregard for the most important product at the core of the business – that most European telecommunications companies were late to invest in 4G.

As soon as we had clarified our innovation playground – pure network telecommunications – we started to hire the best network engineering leaders. I focused on our second-line, as opposed to first-line management. I wanted leaders who were actively involved in messing around with these technologies. People who liked to play with, touch and develop the latest technologies. Engineers who wanted to get their hands dirty.

Very quickly we built an exceptionally strong technology team under a fantastic leader who came from the IT industry. Managers from the IT industry have learned how to develop horizontal solutions, to manage large-scale transformation projects, and to manage partner companies. These capabilities, combined with an incredible passion for delivery, were going to prove essential in developing absolute innovation leadership.

I set up a weekly two-hour meeting with the technology leadership team to discuss, to review, and to brainstorm how we could become the best. The best not just in our country, but globally. We started to look at other regions and operators who were strong in network innovation. We spent many hours researching South Korean telecommunications companies as well as Verizon in the United States and NTT Docomo in Japan. It was extremely useful to step out of our region and review best practices on a global scale. It gave us perspective, inspiration, and allowed us to deeply understand how other technology companies in other markets had become successful.

It was also important to analyse worst practices. I checked out countries in Scandinavia where new 4G network services were introduced but with limited success and uptake. During a visit with my family to Scandinavia, I took the opportunity to visit a few stores that were selling the new 4G services. I reviewed the material, spoke to the staff, and researched the web. It was another fun holiday for my wife. It quickly became clear that the Scandinavians had introduced their new 4G services without enough new compatible smartphones. They had positioned the service more for notebooks and PCs than for surfing the web on a phone. The service was also very expensive and not positioned for the masses.

Back from Scandinavia, with a year to go before our launch date, I immediately prioritized a small, confidential project team to start work on securing long-term 4G smartphone innovation from Apple, Samsung, Nokia, and Microsoft. The team consisted of network engineers, device specialists and handset product managers. We would meet on a regular basis and travel to Asia and the United States to meet key suppliers and partners. We would try to understand their 4G plans and attempt to bring them on board with ours. The Scandinavian experience had helped me drive my own innovation in the right direction. You can learn not just from best practices but also from the ones that have not worked well.

After several meetings, with much activity coalescing around this superfast ideal, we decided that we needed to introduce a new 4G network in the UK as a matter of urgency. This would be the key brand promise of our new company.

4G networks existed in South Korea, the United States, Scandinavia, Japan and a number of other smaller countries, but it was a very new technology in Europe.

Customers hadn't been banging down the door for it and the hurdles were complex and hairy. But often people don't know what they want until they get it. No one had been begging for Wi-Fi in their homes, but within months of it being introduced, it became a fundamental must-have for any self-respecting modern household. It's that old adage attributed to Henry Ford. If he'd told customers about the development of the motorcar they'd have told him they didn't want one – they'd have opted for a faster horse instead.

4G would enable new mobile applications on a smartphone and tablet such as TV, video and mobile commerce, because it enabled speeds that were similar to or higher than what people typically use in some of the best-connected homes in Britain. It would enable customers and businesses to do more with their smartphones in more places. It would truly enable a new, more personal mobile Internet with access to social networks, live TV programmes, and video-rich applications without any buffering. It would reposition our company as a leader in network innovation and customer experience.

But coming up with the idea is much easier than delivering it and we quickly built a list of the hurdles we'd face in delivering our hugely ambitious network plan. I now realize that this list formed a critical component of our success. Innovation is often stalled because something is super hard to do.

Compartmentalizing and rationalizing our challenges in a clear and simple way meant we could pick off each problem one by one quickly and rationally. Some of the issues seemed overwhelming at the time. I often found that delivering on some of the easier quick wins drove team motivation and a belief that we may just pull this off. I never ignored the bigger issues, but found it useful to put them to one side and assign more thinking time to them, while setting the clear expectation among the team that they must, ultimately, be fixed. Never accept a 'no'.

Here was our top list of problems in launching 4G in the timescale we gave ourselves:

1 We can't afford it
In every industry, innovation will incur operating expense, whether that's the engineers themselves, or capital expense such as buying equipment. It is hard to break out of an existing financial model with defined cost and profitability targets. It requires you to believe first and then to convince various stakeholders to invest.

2 We don't have the know-how or capabilities
Here, it is key to identify the people and partners inside or outside of your business who have the knowledge to deliver on what feel like seemingly impossible tasks. Hire them, motivate them, retain them and let them play.

3 The industry has not yet established a standard in this area – if we introduce a new network, there will be no mobile phones available that can use it
In any business where scale and compatibility across different products are key, you need to establish a standard. Some companies will do this through sheer force and size. They will claim the standard (eg Windows from Microsoft). Most companies will have to influence the industry organization that sets standards, and convince the majority of industry players (such as suppliers, competitors and the companies that produce important additional products like accessories or software applications) to drive the industry in the same direction.

4 We do not have the regulatory support to introduce this new technology or new product

A lot of companies in the pharmaceutical, financial services, and utility industries will face the challenges of increasingly powerful regulatory bodies. Your job is to influence the regulator to ensure your project's success (see Chapter 4).

These are specific to our 4G launch, but they're typical hurdles when trying to establish innovation.

Tackling big hurdles

We tackled the first problem in creating the market for 4G – the cost problem – by challenging our unitary cost model. We worked through various suppliers and found companies ready to reduce costs to establish a 'showcase' – a 'first' of new network technologies in the UK. We found new innovative ways to link – and fund – the new project with existing programmes, and to link the new innovation with the old. There was funding for a 2G renewal programme, which required a change of equipment for our many thousands of Orange and T-Mobile antennas. Instead of just renewing the old 2G equipment, we designed a project to visit an antenna once and not just change the old, but install the new 4G equipment and rewire the site – months ahead of our launch schedule. This allowed us to reduce project management, site planning, logistics and engineering costs dramatically. We also developed a clear business case to increase our CAPEX, which our board supported.

To develop the necessary know-how and capabilities, we hired people who had worked on this leading technology in other markets. We secured the best partner companies. We also started to build test environments, labs and trials, to learn and begin demonstrating our innovations in 4G.

Establishing new standards is extremely difficult. Fortunately, we were the largest mobile operator in the UK, so our wishes with our ecosystem partners carried a lot of weight. However, initially, even our size and scale were not enough to convince device manufacturers to support us with 4G-ready handsets, tablets, and other devices.

This meant designing a new sales strategy for these key suppliers. We had our engineers attempting to convince the engineers of our device manufacturers with whitepapers, lab results and trial data. We had our marketeers trying to convince the marketing and sales departments of the device manufacturers with optimistic volume forecasts, exciting marcom plans, and solid go-to-market models. I had to visit every CEO of every company we wanted to work with and push from the top down. We pressed every button. At first, we were not particularly successful. We were only going to secure a few less-than-exciting products from some of the less popular device brands. Some of our larger European network competitors were pushing for a slower timeline and a different underlying technology, unsettling many of the big handset players. So we began using different tactics with the key suppliers.

I asked the engineering teams to compare our requirements with other markets around the world. We identified that our requests were very similar to those in South Korea. This allowed us to simplify and de-risk the work for the device suppliers. By linking our needs with another market, we were finally able to start convincing the major manufacturers, like Apple and Samsung, to move forward and to at least consider an amendment to their roadmaps.

We also decided to take the risk and explain our entire game plan to Apple and Samsung 12 months before launch. On 9 December 2011, I met Apple's CEO Tim Cook and members of his team in Cupertino. We managed to create some real excitement around our plan to capture the UK's imagination with an all-new, market-leading, bold, game-changing strategy. Clearly, Apple and EE share a passion for innovation and for striving to make technology better. It's proof of Tim's excellence as a CEO that he bet on our plan – one that changed the UK industry forever. He took a risk, but Apple has had a larger share of the UK device market than in most European markets ever since.

When we then started to gain alignment with one of our shareholders – Deutsche Telekom in Germany – we secured even more commitment from the device suppliers. Ultimately, this programme was risky for the handset manufacturers. They were all too aware of the obstacles in our way, and so their forecasts were ultimately being linked to our ability to pull off the seemingly impossible. They were especially concerned about the fact that we did not have regulatory support yet, and nervous about upsetting their other customers – our competitors.

My advice is that if you need to secure industry-wide support for your innovation agenda, make sure that you take personal ownership of the challenge and build relationships with industry leaders who have the same ambition and direction as you. In the end, the top-down support from other leaders in their companies will make the difference.

The other key learning for me was to establish true strategic partnerships with key suppliers by taking them into our confidence, sharing our secrets, and by exciting a select number of partners about our purpose and vision. If the supplier has a lot to lose if they do not support you, it can make it easier to get your requirements met.

The challenge of innovation in a big business

Overall, I have learned here and in the IT industry, that developing innovation in a corporate environment is very hard.

Big successful businesses have become big and successful because they have perfected a clear way of doing things. Deviating from that course means risk – and risk is not on the agenda of most big businesses. This 'change = risk' conundrum is at the heart of most decisions that large businesses make, either consciously or unconsciously. Big businesses have a lot to lose if a risk doesn't pay off. Billions of dollars are at stake, and it means that, unfortunately, most businesses and higher education courses teach future managers how to protect *against* risks – not take them.

Of course, the challenge of transformation is that a large supertanker of a company often needs to change in order to stay relevant. But with an army of MBA-trained soldiers, schooled in zero-based budgeting and cost-reduction measures, they simply don't have a team that is educated or incentivized to encourage the required innovation.

Of course, the irony is that innovation is the essence of long-term retained earnings growth. Too many companies drive their share price through dividend payouts and share buybacks rather than driving new revenue and profit development through innovation. The focus on short-term quarterly results inside corporations does not help.

I recommend that if you want to drive innovation through your new business or brand, you first have to find and hire people who would normally not join your corporation. They are less driven by a career, security and development opportunities. They are driven by the freedom and excitement of innovating. Once inside your business, you need to give these individuals the space to develop and to learn. Literally, put an innovation team in a different building, shield it from the corporate processes, procedures and bureaucracy. Innovation requires speed and flexibility.

Not all of their projects will be successful. If they are, they're not pushing the innovation opportunity hard enough. This team must be given permission to fail. The process of managed trial and error – produced in an incubation environment that has zero negative effect on your existing customers – is a proven approach.

You must encourage failure for these small and nimble innovators – otherwise you won't drive true innovation. As the leader, you have to be in the boat with them. You cannot sit on the fence and judge. You have to defend the team against the nay-sayers. You must fail and win together.

Innovation requires a culture where people have the courage to say yes – it's too easy in a corporation for people to say no. Above all, it requires a very different leadership style from the top.

A brand-new DNA – from the inside out

During my career, I have often been sceptical about company values. Too often they are just a few words on a poster. The list is always too long, and – worst of all – the top team does not act in accordance with these values (often this is because they are the values a company aspires to have because they do not exist today).

When I was working at Digital Equipment, I remember an internal poster on the wall that spelled out 'teamwork' in bold letters, written over a photo of a US rowing team on a beautiful river early in the morning with the sun coming up. I love rowing. It's been a passion of mine ever since I learned how to do it in an eight while at Oxford. But as a young product director I hated that poster. Why? Because it was not credible. In that business at that time, there was absolutely no teamwork across the business units. People in other business units – like the Alpha (high-end IT systems) team – openly celebrated when the PC division, with all the youngsters, failed to meet its quarterly targets because of lack of supply.

That's not teamwork. That's stupid.

So a poster doesn't cut it. You must go deeper than that.

When people ask you to remember a job early in your career at a company where you no longer work today, typically you won't remember the exact work, project or task you were responsible for. Instead, you'll more likely remember the atmosphere, some of the people and the general attitude of the business. You remember the cultural attributes of the company or the organization – how it made you feel, how you as a team behaved and acted.

The importance of culture

Cultural values define how a company operates and whether it is fun, engaging and motivating to work there. Company cultures can make or break businesses and are very important. It is typically hard to find one single culture in a company. Normally, there are tribes across the organization. The culture in the sales team is likely to be very different from that of the technology team, or the one portrayed by the back-office staff.

Regardless, it is important to have a small number of core values established everywhere. These central values drive a consistency of behaviour and a level of mutual respect, acceptance and expectation among your people. They can also protect against unethical behaviour by setting expectations, and by establishing an employee-based social control mechanism.

For us, it was essential to bring in a new culture because there were still two – arguably three – distinct employee 'tribes' within the business. Legacy Orange, legacy T-Mobile and now Everything Everywhere employees who had joined since the joint venture began – and that was before you took into account the different big departments within the business such as Sales, Service and Technology.

If we were to truly create one company, with one vision and one way of doing things, we needed ONE culture.

We had the fresh, new, exciting brand that put the network back at the heart of the business and helped customers understand how we could improve their lives through connectivity.

Internally, helping to drive that – and a fundamental part of the EE brand – were our new values.

The importance of company values

Values help define the DNA of a business. They bring the brand to life and drive the behaviours of your people. Defining them is something that should not be done in isolation but, again, in conjunction with your leadership team. The values have to be defined and *lived* by the top team first and foremost. Role-modelling from the leadership team is an essential part of embedding the values within an organization. Because of that, creating these values is hard. Your diverse team will have different definitions of the values and the words you use. They will have different ideas about which values best define the organization you want to become.

Companies will, typically, develop obvious values such as honesty, trust and empathy. You can end up with a very long – and very bland – list. I believe you need to make a difference between values that employees must have to work in your organization, and those that drive the real long-term identity and DNA of the company. The basic values that your employees must have are non-negotiable and can be monitored through Human Resources and the Performance Management Framework. They do not need to be on that poster on the wall.

The true values of your company – the 'DNA values' – should be kept to a minimum. You and your team need to be able to remember them and, more importantly, act in accordance with them. We picked just three – be bold, be clear and be brilliant. They were simple statements that would help guide our people and ensure they understood what was expected of them when serving our customers or in their daily working lives. These are now embedded throughout the organization – from head office, through our call centres, and into every single one of our stores.

They were the simple and powerful values of our company that spoke of action and were designed to be flexible for the different audiences. So, while there was a commonality in the three values, elements of them could also be designed to create certain behaviours or actions relevant to the sales team, or the service team, or the technology team, or whichever team you worked in.

Here are the EE values we put in place:

Be bold

Lead the way like never before

- Stand out, command attention, drive change – always to help make our customers' lives better.
- Surprise people with the unexpected.
- Take initiative in the market and move fast – when we see an opportunity, we make the most of it. We always make sure our customers benefit first from the latest innovations from around the world.
- Keep focused on the things that matter to customers – finding things that are right for them and making technology useful in everyday life.

Be clear

Make digital lives easy to understand

- Say it, make it, do it, tell it – clearly.
- We are transparent with each other. We are straight about the pros and cons of everything, never misleading or hiding important information. We work hard to earn the trust of our customers, day in, day out.
- When it comes to the big industry issues, we're not afraid to take a stand.
- For our customers, we are the people who make this ever-growing world of devices, apps and operating systems simple.
- We absolutely love better ways of doing things, so we get a real kick out of teaching someone else a new skill, and making things better. We pass the good stuff on, and make trying new things and 'having a go' fun and playful.

Be brilliant

Make amazing things happen for everyone in the UK

- We're driven by our passion for the magic of technology and our strong belief that it can benefit everyone, everywhere. Right up and down this country. Whoever or wherever they are.

(*Continued*)

- This is what fires us up each and every moment to make things happen for our customers now.

- So we move fast and we do it brilliantly. Make sure everything is the best it can be. Nothing less than quality is good enough for us. We set the standard with our networks, products and service.

My advice is that it's easier to have a single set of values for your brand inside and out. Getting your employees to live it and love it gives your brand more momentum and more strength in the market.

Once you have your values, the next job is to communicate them to everyone in the organization. You should organize direct communication sessions to share them, discuss your expectations around them, and demonstrate your leadership commitments to them. It is key to ensure that you and your team deliver this at the same time across the entire company. This process secures alignment, common knowledge and the appropriate messaging of the values.

Your brand encapsulates the fundamental essence of what your business is. It is essential you put time, energy and focus on your brand to make sure it resonates emotionally and functionally with your customers.

Ask yourself how important the role of brands is in your industry.

Interrogate your own brand – is it strong enough to address future requirements and to win in new customer segments? If no, you may need to consider a re-sharpening and re-focusing of the brand... or, like us, you may need to introduce a completely new one.

At the end of the day, your brand is more than a logo – it is a promise. Therefore, what you decide to put behind it in terms of product, values, and services is essential.

Getting your employees to live it, love it and understand what it stands for is absolutely key – they are your ambassadors for your brand and your business.

Announcing EE   07

If you are really going to transform an enterprise you've got to understand culture... it took me to age 55 to figure that out. Culture is everything.
LOU GERSTNER, IBM

The following pages will take us through the pre-launch, the launch itself and day one of EE. It was a time of significant pressure and, ultimately, relief and success.

In this chapter, we'll look at how strategic partnerships played a key role in our success, and how detailed project management, military-style communications plans, a significant focus on employee engagement and a cultural revolution inside the business helped us pull off the seemingly impossible.

Managing the pressure points

The summer of 2012 was an incredible moment in time for the UK. It was one of those special periods where you could feel a buzz up and down the nation. The Queen's Diamond Jubilee and the Olympics were creating a sense of unparalleled positivity across the country that even the most cynical among us would find hard to fight.

Over in Paddington, West London, the EE team was locked away from the fervour, working to create its own groundbreaking moment in this special year. Our audacious plan – our big bang – had grown bigger and louder. It was taking shape in exciting new ways and we were itching to press go.

By that summer there were three major components to EE. It was a new company, a new network and a new brand that would sit alongside – and house – Orange and T-Mobile. We created a number of fundamental statements that we were working to as well. We were creating a single, unified company, and were planning to move the business in a number of key ways:

- from former Orange and T-Mobile staff to 15,000 EE employees;
- from legacy values and behaviours to new EE values;
- from two mobile networks to the EE network;
- from Orange and T-Mobile store estates to 700 EE stores, where customers could buy all our products;
- from call centres supporting Orange and T-Mobile to call centres that could handle EE as well;
- from different systems to one way of doing things – the EE way;
- from three strong cultures to one new EE culture.

These were the huge levers that we would have to pull to create the massive transformative change for our customers, our company and our people. Add in the UK's first pioneering 4G service – which would be rolled out to 10 cities on day one, and 16 by the end of the year – and the plan was coming to life.

We were to launch all of this in September. But, for now at least, this was all under wraps. With billions of pounds at stake, the plans for the launch of EE had the same level of secrecy and jeopardy as the two global national events that shared that same special year. Get it right, and the potential of Britain's biggest joint venture in decades would be fulfilled. Get it wrong and… well, it didn't bear thinking about.

The level of attention, speculation and expectation was so vast that every word of every executive was being pawed over by an expectant press. Competitors were desperate to find out what was happening. Employees were starting to hear rumblings that something big was coming down the line. The shareholders were keeping a closer eye on proceedings than ever before. And the politicians and regulators knew that the decisions they made now would have a significant impact on the future of the UK.

In business, the stakes really don't get much higher.

It was in this atmosphere of palpable tension and microscopic attention that we endeavoured to create EE – the UK's biggest communications company, and (at this point) still the industry's biggest secret.

All elements of the team were pulling together to create something special – a once-in-a-lifetime opportunity for many to put their personal mark on the mobile landscape.

We secured complete confidentiality. Back in September 2011, we had started off with 11 people – my leadership team and I. But the trusted few quickly grew, and in the end we had thousands of people under non-disclosure agreements, matching the thousands of lines in the project management file.

Our plan was so outrageously ambitious that most employees who were involved did not believe it was actually possible until a few weeks before launch. Even then, many secretly doubted we would pull it off.

For a whole year we were running two of Britain's best-known brands and, in the background, working on the creation of an entirely different new entrant for the UK market. This was not done by a separate team. It was done by one team delivering business as usual while, behind the scenes, creating the most innovative, inventive and impactful company launch of the past decade. It was extremely exhausting for the senior managers in the company because they had to deliver the running of the business and prepare for our mega launch.

We had ten official projects identified for the company (that brought the Orange and T-Mobile businesses and assets together), along with an eleventh confidential project – the creation of the EE brand. Every Wednesday afternoon, we reviewed the details of the 'Project 11' adventure. Our lead project manager had worked earlier in his career at GCHQ – he knew how to keep secrets.

The art of launch project management

The concept of a 'big bang' – bringing all the key product and service launches together in one major announcement – worked so well for us that we continue to use the same launch methodology today.

Every year, we tried to create one or two major launch dates, where we would bring the entire company together to make a difference in the market with network innovation, new pricing and new partnerships bundled together to maximize impact. When you bring everything together into one integrated launch strategy you save across testing, in project management, in marcoms and in training costs.

A company that has mastered this launch model extremely well is Apple. The engineering, marketing and sales teams drive to a strong and globally consistent big bang, once or twice a year. Unlike most companies, Apple does not waste energy and resources launching major products at multiple times throughout the year. This is a very powerful strategy and requires a lot of discipline in a large-matrix organization.

But it's complex. So how did we do it?

The key to our success was in dedicated, 100 per cent focused professional project management. We mapped every sub-project, coordinated every step, and secured quality across the board.

Project management resources can be found externally, but I prefer to have a strong pool of experienced individuals inside the business. You need them for a large-scale transformation. They need to be able to maneuver inside your company and establish strong relationships across the organization – a much easier job when they are on the inside.

One of the things that helped tremendously was the linkage between all the sub-projects and a common milestone – the one date, one time, one place when we would launch all together at once… the big bang. This created an interdependency and sense of urgency, which I have not seen before. It became a permanent competition between the work streams and had a hugely positive impact and outcome for the individuals involved, not to mention the project itself.

It created a tight bond within the wider delivery team – a feeling of real camaraderie. We all had purpose. We were all working toward a common goal.

In early summer, following months of trial and error, the IT team had to admit defeat on a major part of our plan. They realized they could not deliver the integration of our point-of-sale systems into the newly furnished stores for our planned September launch. The integration of a legacy Orange and T-Mobile point-of-sale system simply required too much re-coding and testing. It was a significant blow. But instead of compromising the launch and leaving this crucial element out, we decided to delay all elements of the big bang by four weeks. Everything else was lined up and ready to go. But this one item simply wasn't ready. We did not allow one work stream to break out on a different timeline. We were in it together. A few days before launch, we continued to have IT challenges and the new date was at risk again. The IT work stream worked day and night to get it back under control – and they did. It was absolutely amazing.

Everyone had their own part to play, and everyone pulled together to make it happen.

There is no plan B

It was a time of real tension and nervousness among the project teams. Many of our projects and sub-projects were marked as red or amber on the status report. There were very few – if any – greens right up until the week before launch. People would ask me during the most difficult delivery board meetings: 'What's our plan B?' 'There is no plan B', I would say. 'There is only one plan delivered by everyone in time for the busiest trading season in the year. The final golden quarter. If we miss it, we have failed in our first major step in the transformation of this business.'

These are demanding times – demanding on the business, and demanding on yourself. As the leader, it is critical that you believe in the project's success. You have to drive it. It is your project. If it fails, you are accountable. You have to immerse yourself in the details. When there are failures and setbacks, you have to motivate yourself and your team, and help find the way through.

The hardest elements of your plan are those you cannot control yourself. In my case, this was to get regulatory approval to launch a new network. We had been putting our case forward for almost a year. We wanted to build a 4G network, using our existing assets and outside of the government's proposed timetable. Our competitors had used every legal trick in the book to try to stop us. They'd thrown everything at it. All of their competitive energy seemed to be spent on legal tools rather than innovation.

It was so hard to remain optimistic during this period, but it was essential to show the team confidence through the setbacks and self-doubt. As a leader you cannot show your own doubts about a transformation project you have set in motion.

Really, the only people you can share your doubts with are the ones on the outside of the business – your partner, a mentor, a member of your family, or your best friend. They will often be people from different backgrounds who have handled large-scale transformations themselves, and who can coach and support you.

Out of hours, I would confide in two highly experienced former CEOs – people who had done it all and seen it all. I met them individually and in private every few months. I tested my ideas with them. They challenged them and helped me shape them. I shared my most confidential questions with them and they fed back openly and honestly. It helped me tremendously. It was essential to have these sounding boards in a time of such immense pressure.

The clock was ticking to get this thing away. Our original launch for EE was the end of September. Having pushed it back once already due to the IT sales integration issue, we did not have the luxury of doing so again.

Our new launch date was set for the end of October 2012. We now had just 10 weeks until launch day. Although most of the project was marked as amber or red, things were generally on track. All, that was, except one fundamental element – the one thing that remained out of our control. The approval for our launch of 4G. We were still waiting on the word from the regulator.

This went to the wire. For us at least. Of course, no one else knew just how critical it was for us to get approval to launch 4G in the timeframe we had mapped out. No one else knew just what was riding on it. Without 4G, we were launching nothing more than a logo. No product, no differentiation, no innovation.

On the evening of 20 August 2012, I was in my apartment in Richmond, South West London. My family was travelling. I received a phone call around 8 pm from my head of public and regulatory affairs. He spoke slowly and clearly, informing me that we had received the letter to confirm that our application to use our existing spectrum to launch our new 4G services had been approved. I could not believe it. The weight on my shoulders from months of waiting and fighting began to disappear. It was the only project I could not entirely control myself. We could lobby government, work the legal side, and drive positive public opinion. But ultimately the decision was in the hands of people who did not work for me or my shareholders. I was so stunned I had to lie down outside on the balcony floor! The relief was overwhelming. We were a GO.

The importance of strategic partnerships

EE's success was not just down to its brilliant employees. It was also down to thousands of people who worked for our suppliers. We galvanized these groups of people by bringing them in on the secrets and the opportunities that lay ahead with success. We grew our army by turning our suppliers into strategic partners.

In doing this, you need to analyse a few key issues. First of all, you have to review all of your key suppliers and understand the financial drivers. How big are you for them, and vice versa? Are they a customer as well as a supplier? What is the potential future position of *their* spend and *your* buying? Having established the financial overview, you need to understand the strategic importance of the supplier in your portfolio for the short and medium term.

This analysis will lead to some simple prioritization. Typically, you will need to create a tiered system. Each partnership tier has a different importance, a different agenda, a different time span and different money invested. When you go through this, you will find that your organization spends far too much time and energy on its tier two and tier three partners. Mostly, this is because of history. Often, you'll find that the partnership used to be really important but is less so today. A great example of this for us was the once-giant Nokia. Within our business – and theirs – there were established relationships and programmes. It is key to reduce efforts on tier two and three partners in order to unleash real energy on tier one. Only tier one is truly strategic.

Once you've mapped this out, you have to establish the real status of the tier one relationships. How many critical people do we know in the company? Do we know their plans? Do we regularly meet and review the performance of the buying and the supplier relationship? Do we have a common go-to-market plan and regular reviews? Does our contract reflect a partnership or a pure commodity relationship? Is the relationship following a purely legal or contractual agenda? Does the company seek strategic partnerships or not?

Sometimes, you can have a critical supplier with whom it is absolutely impossible to build a strategic partnership because they – not you – are in an exceptionally strong position (an example of this in the PC world would be Microsoft or Intel). Or perhaps they are just structured in too complicated a way to partner successfully (as we found with Google). Or maybe they are simply not interested.

Once, I tried to create a strategic partnership with GoPro to develop and launch 4G-connected cameras. They did not even return my phone calls or my e-mails, so in the end we developed our product without them. Sometimes you have to accept that the people you want to date just won't turn up for dinner.

At EE, we decided to strengthen and build far-reaching tier one partnerships with Apple, Samsung, Sony, Huawei and BT – they spanned the two all-important challenges we had... building our network and ensuring we had first-class devices that would work on it.

We did not establish dedicated partnership account managers. Instead, we made sure that one of the chiefs from our top team owned the overall partnership. He or she owned and organized the overall strategic relationship. In the IT industry, I used to build dedicated teams. This is expensive and can end up costing a business a lot of extra – and unnecessary – money. Clearly, you should only do this if the strategic partner is a large customer as well. In that case, it's easy to establish the strategic partnership within the account team.

Driving competitive differentiation through strategic partnerships

If you do not have a strong relationship with the CEO of a strategic partner, you will have a hard time in driving a true partnership. I met the CEOs of my partner companies face to face at least twice a year and communicated regularly with them. Our strategic partner companies knew my confidential company roadmap for the next 12 to 24 months. I knew their key plans too. We discussed things and established formal combined partnership plans that included technical, marketing, sales, purchasing and financial activities. These plans had clear joint goals and objectives.

Ultimately, strategic partnerships are built through strong relationships right across the company, starting with you. It is not complicated, but a lot of companies do not have a partnering culture, and too many people in your organization will not understand the difference between a supplier or buyer, and a strategic partner.

Many companies that do not have a partnering culture often believe they can do it all. They don't need a partnership with a software company because they have their own software engineers. They don't need to partner with indirect resellers because they have their own shops. Partnering also means defining what your company does not excel at or cannot do alone. You will have to show the way here. Many of your team will be too proud to admit they need help.

Without our strategic partners, we would not have been able to make a difference in innovation. Some of the relationships were so strong that my chief technology officer would be able to call upon the top management day or night to help accelerate the rollout of 4G. I would have the CEO on the phone throughout the weekend.

While not as *strategically* important, our tier two and tier three partners also played important roles in delivering on the innovation. We created an over-arching programme with these companies. They were informed about parts of the plans, they knew our vision and what we needed to achieve. They understood their position and accountabilities in the overall team and these were clarified regularly. Finally, a tight governance and project management structure was put in place. Where possible, we also tried to co-locate representatives from each of the companies to ensure alignment and teamwork. Areas that were super critical – or those that did not deliver – would be managed through a 'war room' model with even tighter governance, control and dedicated technical support. At its pinnacle over 5,000 people were working seven days a week around the clock, tightly controlled through a central project and programme management team. But the direct engagement and passion of my CTO was the most important ingredient. If you want to bring technical innovation to your business, the technology leader needs to be passionate, energetic and obsessively dedicated.

At one point during the rollout of our 4G network, I had a hard time sleeping. Progress simply wasn't fast enough. We were supposed to launch in October with a couple of thousand antennae. This would give us enough coverage in 10 key cities. We had to add 20 to 30 antennae a day but we were in single digits. It was frightening. Equipment would be installed but the new kit would not connect properly. There were always issues like the cables being incorrectly connected. We simply did not activate sites fast enough. In the middle of yet another sleepless night, I called my CTO. He too was awake, and answered the phone immediately. I told him that I could not sleep any more with this lack of progress. He replied, 'Me too!' He committed that he would make it happen from this point onwards and that he would introduce night shifts. 'I don't need to sleep much anyway', he said. He personally project managed the day and night shifts with reviews early in the mornings as we headed toward our launch day. He also created a permanent war room to supervise and correct issues in installation and setup. He was absolutely committed to go the extra 10 miles to keep a promise of delivery. If you do not have passionate and courageous leaders like that in your organization, large-scale transformation is impossible.

The communications challenge

There were still a few lumps and bumps in the plan, but with our network rolling out across the country, handsets being readied in factories across the world, a brand coming to life before our very eyes, and the structure of a new business being built behind the scenes, we were now speeding towards launch. The plan to tell our people, our customers and the world about EE was well and truly in action.

We had a clear three-point structure for this final piece of the jigsaw. We would 'break cover' and tell the world six weeks before launch, bring in our employees, suppliers and dealers during those six weeks, then launch. It was a model that we would be able to shift depending on the actual date of launch – now set for 30 October. Having taken that fateful call on 20 August, that meant we now had just over 20 days to get everything ready to announce EE to an unexpectant public.

Here's the timetable we set for the public launch of EE:

- **10 September:** Pre-break cover. We would reveal our plans to the store and call centre managers of our internal front-line teams, our leadership team, key third parties, and analysts – all under embargo for 24 hours.

- **11 September:** Official break cover. We would announce EE and our plans publicly for the first time to customers, press and our people.

- **21 September:** 4G-ready devices would go on sale.

- **9–15 October:** Every single employee would go through a fully immersive brand experience.

- **23 October:** Detailed information about EE tariffing and products would be made available.

- **30 October:** EE would launch. All 700 EE stores would reveal a newly re-branded look, our advertising would go live and EE would be available to buy for the first time.

It was a well-planned, well-executed communications plan that exploited maximum interest and excitement about the launch, built on the belief of 'tell them it's coming, tell them it's here, tell them how good it is… then tell them all over again'.

Breaking cover

The week of 10 September was our big reveal.

Even though all of my business chiefs – and many of our directors – had been working for over a year on our plans, ensuring that we had just one version of 'the truth' of EE was absolutely key. There could be no cracks, and making sure that everyone was aligned on a single set of messaging about who we were, what we stood for, why we were doing this and what made us different, was an essential final piece of this gigantic ever-shifting puzzle.

After months of work on the positioning and messaging, we finally nailed it on the evening of Sunday 9 September, just hours before we were to bring our first front-line employees into the fold.

Bringing our people in first was a big risk. The potential of a leak was huge. But I believe that if you respect your people with big news, they will respect the business with that information.

The stage was set at the Science Museum in London – a fitting launch pad replete with examples of humankind's quest for innovation and adventure.

In the amphitheater were an imposing black stage and a rising bank of 500 seats that would soon be full of eager and excited employees. They would be the first to hear the story of EE and our plans to change the industry.

The auditorium was filled to capacity with 500 store managers chattering to each other, brimming with anticipation. Patched in by phone were a further 200 store managers from across the country who couldn't join in person due to shift patterns (a fitting example of one of the hardest elements in the run up to launch EE – namely, making sure that our existing businesses carried on ticking over and that trading was not compromised in any way).

The lights went down and our chief sales officer Marc Allera stepped onto the stage to introduce the session. He explained to our audience that everything they were going to hear today had been a secret for 12 months – and that we needed them to continue to keep it a secret for just 24 hours more. The tension was building. Marc then introduced me onto the stage. I recall the single, searing emotion that I felt – pure excitement. We had built up to this moment for over a year – and it was a year of pretty much solid work. Eighteen-hour days, seven-day weeks. Now, finally, we were in a position to reveal what we had been working toward.

I took the team through the journey we had all been on, setting the context for why we were here. I talked about our two brands, Orange and T-Mobile, about serving 27 million customers day in, day out. And I talked about our network, and how we'd worked hard to build out the best 2G and 3G coverage in Britain. And then, the big reveal:

> Tomorrow, we will unveil a new name for our company – the company we all work for. We are to be called EE. We are also unveiling a new network, the biggest and best in the UK, with unique services that no other company can offer. Our network is to be called EE. And we will also be launching a new customer brand – a brand that will sit at the heart of people's digital lives, built for 21st-century Britain and born in a digital age. This brand will stand alongside Orange and T-Mobile and is called EE.

And tomorrow is the day we share our plans to launch 4G – the fourth-generation superfast mobile service that will revolutionize our industry.

My session then ended with a few closing words:

So this is big. This is a massive change for us. A massive change for our industry. And a massive change for our customers. And we are all leading it. You will be leading it all from tomorrow. Congratulations – you are taking us into the future.

On handing back to Marc you could feel the buzz in the room. The brand had been revealed on giant screens and the proposition we were putting forward was hugely compelling – a new company with a unique service that could not be matched by the competition. The room was fit to burst.

It was a wonderful moment.

Just five minutes later, however, disaster almost struck. Every key detail of everything I had just revealed – and everything that Marc was saying up there on stage at that very moment – was being tweeted by one of our employees.

Welcome to the social media revolution!

Dramatically, Marc was stopped mid-flow and told of the situation. He took a moment to compose himself before explaining to the audience what had happened in the gravest of terms. He spoke of broken trust and disappointment. The crowd were equally disappointed that one of their number had seemingly broken ranks and let the cat out of the bag.

Behind the scenes, our communications team was desperately trying to trace the rogue tweeter and stop them. Within just a few minutes, the tweet had been tracked to the account of a part-time retail employee. His store manager had left the conference call dial-in details on a Post-it note on the screen of the store computer and, in his curiosity, the employee had dialed in halfway through my speech, missing Marc's request for total confidentiality.

Once he had been traced and the severity of the situation explained to him, he immediately removed his tweets and remorsefully apologized.

It was not malicious, just silly. This was the scoop that every journalist from every national newspaper had wanted for years – the true and final revelation about the joint venture. And for 20 minutes it was out there for all to read – but no one spotted it.

It was a lucky escape, but also vindication for our people that, aside from one rogue unwanted guest, the trust between employees and the corporation had held.

Once Marc had closed the session, our people filed out, bouncing off the walls with excitement. This story was now theirs to share and to make successful. They left the Science Museum knowing that from tomorrow, their secret could be told.

The next day, 100 journalists filed into those exact same seats and sat in anticipation of what was to come (perhaps not *quite* as excited and eager as our people the day before... this was the British media after all).

It was a spectacular scene and a real sign of how times had changed since the formation of the joint venture. All the journalists had a laptop or tablet out in front of them and were filing their stories as the conference took place. The news of EE broke in real time. It was a powerful sign of the digital revolution in action and we knew that soon they would be using our 4G network – not a boosted Wi-Fi signal – to do that from some of the remotest parts of Britain and the world.

On 11 September 2012 at 10 am, the news of EE was announced. Our big bang was out, loud and proud. We revealed that:

- EE would become the UK's biggest digital communications network, serving 27 million customers.
- EE would launch as a new company, a new network and a new customer brand.
- EE would launch as the company's 'superfast' brand with the UK's first 4G mobile service and fibre in the home.
- EE would be a consumer and business brand.
- EE would be our exclusive broadband brand.
- EE would become the device network and broadband indicator for all our customers.
- 4G mobile services – offering five-times-faster speeds – would be launched in 16 cities this year, with a third of the British population covered by Christmas. 4G would continue to be

rolled out throughout 2013 and beyond in towns and cities in rural areas.

- EE would reinvent pricing for the digital age, with unlimited voice calls and texts for free – customers simply choose a data package that's right for them.

- A large 4G device range would be available at launch, including household names Samsung, HTC, Nokia – with more to come soon (this was a veiled reference to Apple's impending launch of their new iPhone just 24 hours later… EE would be the first UK operator to launch a 4G version of the device).

- There would be 10,000 experts on hand to help EE, Orange and T-Mobile customers – on the phone, online and in more than 700 EE stores on Britain's high streets.

Now that's a big bang.

We had also enlisted the services of London Mayor Boris Johnson. As with all politicians, we weren't sure he was actually going to turn up until the very last minute, but three-quarters of an hour into the session, and just minutes before he was due to go on stage, he arrived. He was immediately ushered on and expounded the virtues of London and 4G, freely admitting that he hadn't got a clue what it was all about but that if it was good for London, it was good for him! He was a fantastic, verbose orator, who brought the room to life and was a great closing act for the premier of our launch.

At the same time, across our numerous sites from Greenock right down to Plymouth, our employees were able to engage with the excitement too, a huge internal reveal taking place in our buildings, centres and stores. Staff could patch in live to the press conference, and a full internal communications assault began across every site.

The company's new website – ee.co.uk – went live, giving everybody a chance to see and understand what EE was, and, importantly, the chance to register their interest to join the UK's first 4G network in advance of its launch in October.

We were now able to talk directly with our customer base too. Orange and T-Mobile customers needed our reassurance and a complete understanding of what this announcement meant for them.

It kick-started a stream of customer communications as we headed towards the launch itself.

Later in the day we spoke with our key corporate customers and suppliers, introducing them to EE too.

We also knew that the role of the front-line managers was critical. The shift operation of our business was complex and people on early shifts had to be briefed before they opened their stores or started to settle in to take customer calls.

It was huge. Epic. A mammoth task, executed with precision.

Launch success through employee engagement

The reaction to our plans was exactly what we had hoped.

Our employees were buzzing, excited and couldn't wait to get going. The press were interested, positive and generally on-side – a massive turnaround from the years of negative stories and attitudes that felt like we were being consistently set up to fail. And, most importantly, our customers were intrigued and wanted to find out more about this big company with the strange small name and curious new superfast service dubbed '4G'.

Along with all the traditional communications channels, we also installed a social media 'war room' to manage EE's instant relationship with customers, detractors and competitors. It delivered incredible results, engaging people at every turn with the new brand and our new plans.

We had been determined to make EE a digital brand for a digital age, and we lived that through our social media contact with customers.

Twitter, Facebook and digital PR were all used to drive awareness of EE weeks before the traditional marketing campaign began. We were having conversations with our customers over social channels within minutes of having announced our plans at the Science Museum. Kevin Bacon was still six weeks away.[20]

Just days after our announcement, there was a 20 per cent awareness of EE and a 13 per cent consideration to buy through digital and earned-media channels alone. This was before we'd spent a single penny on traditional media placement. In fact, we were still weeks away from anyone being able to buy an EE product in store. '4GEE' hit 12.7 million trend impressions before the week was out and the team at Twitter proclaimed these as great results, explaining that 'EE have managed to smash every benchmark we have'.

And the week one rollercoaster didn't end there. Just a day after launch, at 6 pm UK time, EE went truly global.

For months, I had been holding confidential meetings with Apple to secure a key hero handset for our 4G launch – the new iPhone. Working with our engineers, Apple had ensured that special 4G sims would work in their phones to enable our customers to use 4G on their favourite handset.

It was clear at the Apple launch that the 4G version of their iPhone was only available on EE, and the EE logo shone up on an image of Europe for all the world to see. The EE brand was literally on the map – not bad for a company that was only 24 hours old.

As for the brand itself, reaction was generally positive – certainly there was a collective sigh of relief from everyone involved that Everything Everywhere had been ditched for the easier-to-use EE. Even the journalists were pleased – no more arguments with their sub-editors about trying to fit Everything Everywhere into a headline! Some compared the logo to Mr Peanut, others said it was reminiscent of the quiz board from the classic British TV show Blockbusters (I wouldn't know – I'm Dutch), but aside from some gentle jibing, it was quickly adopted as the go-to brand for superfast services in the UK.

Inside the business too, this crucial week was the raising of the flag that enabled us to move from the greyness of Everything Everywhere to the bold, clear and brilliant new EE brand, with its vibrant aqua and yellow colours. We invested significant time, money and resources to make our business a better place to work, with a new way of doing things, new facilities and new employee benefits for our people.

From the buildings where we worked, to new e-mail addresses, from the way we referred to ourselves, to what our pay slips looked like – things started to look and feel different, fresh and new. In these situations, it's the little things that count – not just the big statements. Removing the grey became an obsession of mine over the coming months.

From e-mail signatures to business cards, screensavers to fonts, the quicker you can transform the visible elements of your brand, the quicker your transformation will occur.

We are EE

To call the activity that took place over the coming six weeks between our big reveal and launch 'a flurry' would be the biggest understatement. It was manic. The clock was ticking toward launch and so much was still to be done.

However, having the burden of the EE secret now lifted from the team's shoulders was hugely motivating, and right across the company our people truly embraced the superfast ideal.

Employees worked above and beyond, and issues that had previously seemed critical and fatal to the project were miraculously overcome and delivered on. I believe this was because of the power of what had been revealed – everybody wanted to be a part of it. We had created a movement with real momentum, and we were heading toward the 30 October with confidence and pride.

In the weeks before launch, we took every employee – all 15,000 of them – through a massive immersion experience called EE Live. For many, it was the first time they were able to properly engage with the brand that had been revealed to them on a poster or through a video some weeks earlier.

The event itself was as innovative as our brand. We used exciting new technologies such as Musion – a 3D 'hologram' technology – to amaze our people while ensuring they remained engaged in the key messaging and requests that we were offering up to them. It was essential that the leadership team shared and lived the brand with all our employees. As the full leadership team could not be at the event for the full two weeks (they were both gearing up to launch *and* running our two existing brands), the communications team used life-sized holographic avatars of each of the chiefs instead. Each one presented their function and role in the new company. It was an amazing experience. There was always at least one chief actually present but the others were incredibly real 3D holograms. It always took the audience a few minutes to realize that the team wasn't physically present. It was an absolutely amazing show that ended in a big hall where people could experience 4G, the new product and services, and the brand itself.

Our employees were made to feel like *participants* in the story of the brand with the creation of an EE world that brought 4G and the new company to life.

This was employee engagement on an industrial scale, and after 25 sessions held at the NEC arena in Birmingham, our troops were ready to serve our customers and extol the virtues of EE.

On 23 October – a week before launch – we announced more detail about our tariffs and product set. We held this back as long as possible to ensure we retained as much competitive advantage as we could. If we had gone earlier, it would have given our competitors a chance to react and spoil the party.

Launching mobile price plans that were available from as little as £30, we told our people:

> From next week we will offer our customers a new way to connect to the people, places and things they want on the move, with speeds five times faster than today's mobile technologies. They'll benefit from superfast speeds, smart new services, simple pricing and expert service for consumers and businesses.

We boldly claimed that we were reinventing pricing for the digital age, with unlimited voice calls and texts for free – customers would simply choose the data package that was right for them.

We talked about speeds like no other, enabling connectivity five times faster on the move with 4G, and eight times faster in homes and offices with fixed-line fibre broadband.

We revealed smart new services such as the EE film store, which gave you a free film to download each week on the move, plus the promise of expert service with instant access to our 10,000 front-line people on the high street, on the phone and online, as well as Clone Phone – our add-on service that enabled us to replace your device and all of your digital content in under 24 hours if it got lost, stolen or broken.

On 29 October, we found ourselves on the eve of the biggest business launch any of us had ever been involved with.

Most of our stores had already had a secret EE makeover. Once the brand had been locked down in the summer, we had secretly installed the EE livery in hundreds of stores across the country, then re-papered temporary Orange or T-Mobile branding over the top without even the store staff knowing. It meant that we could deliver the big reveal to full effect on launch day. Thousands of new uniforms were winging their way across the UK to put the finishing touch to the big day.

We also re-branded every element of our HQ and contact centre sites – from the stationery and systems to the workplace itself.

We switched off our intranet and launched a new EE internal social network – a real signal of the digital nature of our new company. For the first time, it enabled all of our people – wherever they worked in the business – to talk to each other, share ideas and support neighbouring departments.

We introduced a new single knowledge system for our front-line employees, giving them access to everything they needed to serve our customers across all three of our brands.

And, of course, our team of brilliant engineers officially switched on our 10 inaugural 4G cities – London, Manchester, Birmingham, Bristol, Cardiff, Edinburgh, Leeds, Liverpool, Sheffield and Glasgow.

EE was born.

In every sense, the launch of EE was an onslaught on the rest of the industry. A tour de force of planning and delivery, it was the product of teamwork, hard work, imagination, belief and smart thinking. In the run-up to launch we sometimes rolled the dice. Occasionally we had to paper over the cracks. Business is never simple and is rarely a smooth endeavour. But on 30 October 2012, we launched EE – the UK's first 4G network, and the culmination of the country's biggest joint venture of the new millennium.

We took 34,000 lines of a project plan and turned them into EE, becoming a major force to be reckoned with in British business in the process.

If you are in the midst of planning, developing, and executing a bold new plan for your business, ask yourself – do you have the best in-house project management driving the plan? Successful project management can help you to deliver things within time, drive cost benefits, and can give a boost to overall employee morale.

Do you have the right partnerships with the right people in place? If your business does not have the scale or the control of the whole value chain in your industry, strategic partnering can be instrumental for your bold new plan. Successful partnering will start at the top and relies on open, transparent and confidential relationships.

Launching the outcome of your plan both internally and externally is the opportunity for you to create true momentum with employees and customers. The way you launch will also define the ambition and the identity of your project.

For the EE team, getting this far was a monumental achievement. But the hard work had only just begun...

The challenge of momentum 08

Business is like riding a bicycle. Either you keep moving or you fall down.
FRANK LLOYD WRIGHT

This chapter is all about the morning after the night before.

Having spent months building toward that moment of transformation, and having launched your big bang, the biggest challenge still awaits – how do you keep things moving?

Transformation typically involves significant changes in IT requirements and systems. With changes in IT, there is often major impact on your back office and your customer interface in shops, through distribution partners, over the web, and over the phone.

A fantastic marketing and sales plan will fail unless you have IT and customer services under control. In this chapter, I'll share my learnings in these key areas. I will also discuss the importance of evolving your core capability, using the EE network as an example.

2013 and 2014: the superfast years

So far in this book, we've looked at the years in the run-up to launching EE, and the launch itself.

But after the exhilaration of creating a new business that's pioneering and positive in its actions, you face the challenge of how to keep the adrenalin of your company pumping.

How do you ensure 15,000 people remain engaged, energized, motivated and delivery-focused?

How do you keep things fresh and evolve the story without contradicting the past?

This is where transformation becomes really tough. You've painted the vision, you've launched the brand, now people need to feel and live the change constantly – and there's a huge amount of heavy lifting that goes with that.

For EE, if 2012 was the year of creation, then 2013 was the year of acceleration.

That's not to say that everything was perfect. It wasn't. Launching a new business is not an exact science. Often it consists of a series of trade-offs that you have to make to reach the best possible outcome for your customers and your company. For EE, areas such as customer services had to cope with a lot of change that ultimately resulted in a poor experience for some of our critical early adopters. This was a huge problem for us – and, of course, for our customers themselves. The team worked hard to resolve the issues, but seemingly simple (although internally hugely complex) issues, such as getting accurate bills out to our customers, would haunt us in our first few months of trading.

That's where we'd got to with EE. We'd done everything our time and money could afford us to create the best possible experience for our customers and make the biggest possible impact on the market.

It wasn't perfect, but we had got the launch away and, generally, things were working. Certainly, the vast majority of our customers were dazzled by the speed of our service and more were piling in to experience the power of 4G every day. The EE customer base accelerated as our 4G rollout continued. We had over half a million people using the service by the summer of 2013, and as we switched on the network in more towns and cities, more people were finding out what 4G could do for them.

Driving change in customer behaviour

Our insight into customer behaviours showed a huge rise in social media and video usage, fuelled by the new service.

One in four Britons were checking social media apps more than 10 times a day on their 4G smartphone or tablet, and people were sharing videos and pictures over 4G, meaning that, on our network, upload traffic had overtaken download traffic at key national events for the first time.

4G wasn't just a new product or service, it was a cultural and behavioural shift in the way that people were accessing their digital lives on the move.

People were using it to share, to send and to stream, with one in three 4G users accessing more video services (such as BBC iPlayer, Netflix and Sky Go) than they did on 3G.

And 71 per cent of our 4G users were shopping on their smartphone or tablet.

The majority of early adopters of 4G were male (although more women would adopt the service in the months to come), with 18–34-year-olds making up the majority of our initial base.

Because 4G provided consistency as well as fast speeds, customers were increasingly using it to replace public Wi-Fi and home broadband – this trend accelerated as we rolled out 4G to less urban areas that had fewer public Wi-Fi hotspots and relatively poor home broadband speeds. In fact, our research showed that by the summer of 2013, 43 per cent of our 4G users were using fewer or no public Wi-Fi hotspots, and 23 per cent were using their home broadband less.[21]

We also witnessed major changes in behaviour during significant cultural moments for the country.

On the day of Margaret Thatcher's funeral, for instance, uploading exceeded downloading in the area of St Paul's Cathedral. This was likely fuelled by people viewing the funeral procession, taking pictures and videos and uploading them to social media sites.

And during the London Marathon we saw a huge peak in upload activity around Greenwich Park – the area runners congregate before the race – as competitors uploaded images of themselves on social media sites.

Andy Murray's victory at Wimbledon, which saw him become the first British man to win in over 70 years, also saw an interesting shift in behaviour. It was a sunny day, and the network handled a huge peak in traffic – 20 per cent higher than any day before on the 4G network – as tennis fans watched Murray's historic victory live on their phones in parks and gardens around the country.

And six months in, the brand was performing well too. In a short space of time, EE's brand awareness was already high, with nearly three-quarters of people aware of EE when prompted. And as for spontaneous awareness, EE was already up there with Virgin, Three and Tesco Mobile. However, it was still some way behind O2 and Vodafone.[22]

Regardless, we had seriously impacted our competitors in the market. Consumer consideration for mobile brands showed that, in the fourth quarter of 2012, every single one of our competitors' brands took a hit on consideration due to EE's launch.[23]

We had shaken up the market, and were known – and bought – for 4G. Our customer community was growing. We were attracting quality connections and winning top business accounts.

However, there was still much more to do.

We had no Pay as you Go offer and our network rollout – fast as it was – still hadn't reached all corners of the UK. We were not yet available to everyone. We were very much seen as providing a premium service that was not affordable to all. It was also hard to convince everyone about 4G when our competitors were downplaying its relevance. In addition, while the vast majority of our customers were happy with the network performance, a number of them were dissatisfied with the quality of our customer service across our physical and digital platforms.

We had done as much as we could to get EE up and running. We did a good job, but there was significantly more to do.

Our network needed to continually innovate, our IT needed a boost, our service experience needed an overhaul and our sales team had to radically evolve if it was to deliver true momentum in 4G.

A technological transformation

One of the key areas that needed changing at EE – both before the launch and in the years that followed – was IT. For a technology company, that's a rather rough thing to have to admit, but quite simply, our IT – both for our people and our customers – was just not good enough.

I have worked in the IT industry for almost 20 years and I do not remember a single company that did not have complaints from both employees and customers about their IT system, costs, or processes. In my view, IT is one of the hardest – and most visible – areas to get right, because it is the technological mirror image of your business. Every single business decision triggers an IT response because every business is dependent on digital processes and systems. Even farming is IT-centric nowadays. I remember meeting a farmer in Austria who measured his cows using digital 3D scanners that used light instead of lasers to protect the animal. He could measure the effectiveness of different feeding and resting regimes to develop the optimal milk production! Literally IT in the field!

The IT at EE was really bad. The people were good but there were several problems that all converged at the same time. Our systems were too old. They had suffered from under-investment for some years. If you touched them, they would fall over. Some systems were so old that we dared not switch them off in case they didn't re-boot! The people who understood the software were reaching retirement. Did they at least have instruction manuals? No. Unfortunately, it was like that old TV system guide that disappeared behind the sofa a long time ago. We had very limited documentation about processes and software. We also had a mixed bag of suppliers with different service level agreements, that typically did not meet our end-to-end requirements. We had too many uncontrolled changes requested from the business that resulted in disastrous outages. Our incident management system did not work. The list of problems went on and on.

So how do you improve your IT? Clearly, like any area, you need a strong leader.

Information technology lessons learned the hard way

The best CIO I ever met in my career was a guy called Randy Mott. In my opinion, he was the rock star of the IT industry because he was able to articulate and manage an IT strategy that was 100 per cent aligned to the business results. The business in this case was HP. He had been responsible for developing the scalable IT architecture at Walmart and Dell and had an amazing ability to simplify and streamline complexity. He was also able to translate an IT strategy into both P&L and share price benefits. During his first presentation at HP, he demonstrated how his IT plan would boost the share price through cost reduction and a better time-to-market capability. He was incredibly straightforward and clear. I learned a lot from him.

Information Week described him as follows:

> Mott's HP years, from 2005 to 2011... were marked by massive cost cutting and consolidation, as CEO Mark Hurd tapped him to reduce the company's IT spending from 4 per cent of revenue to 2 per cent.

Essentially, he succeeded in delivering on his promises through a significant IT simplification effort. He shortened the list of IT priorities in every business. He reduced the number of data centres. He removed a large number of applications. He moved to a single enterprise data warehouse. He centralized IT cost control and purchasing. These efforts freed up resources and energy to focus on the very selective development of new stuff. The key to success was to reduce the maintenance of old stuff and to increase investments in the new.

Apart from his capability and know-how, Randy was successful because the leader of HP, Mark Hurd, empowered him from day one. Mark allowed him to get full line of sight and signatory responsibility on every bit of IT, right across the business. This is crucial to getting good results. I recommend you apply the same model to avoid shadow IT budgets and create an environment of transparency and control in an area that most people in a company believe they can master.

Here are a few powerful quotes from Randy Mott, which I will never forget and still apply in my world:

The average shelf life of a CEO... the CIO's boss... is four years. So if your IT plan does not deliver significant results in years two and three, you'd better change it from the start.

If an IT project cannot deliver within a 12-month period, it means the scope is too complicated. Businesses change all the time. Therefore, your scope will change all the time and your IT project will never deliver.

Every business decision triggers an IT response. If you have too many IT projects and IT costs, you have to prioritize the IT projects at the highest level of the company. Too many CEOs do not understand the IT roadmap, and do not know what they're signing off.

If you want to save money, avoid investing in the latest Information Technology buzzword first (cloud, outsourcing, CRM, etc). These buzzwords often mean profit for your supplier and big, lengthy projects for your company.

Every company has IT challenges. A strong CIO like Randy can open doors by sharing best IT practices. His IT transformation plan was so impressive that he delivered great support to the sales people in the business-to-business team, ultimately helping them to create more meaningful partnerships – and business – with key large accounts.

So how do you structure an IT transformation when you are the CEO of a large firm?

The key challenge is to articulate the issues you are trying to resolve. Typically, they fall into three categories: our IT costs too much, our IT is unstable, and our IT is too slow to truly create a competitive advantage. Obviously, in many companies, it's a combination of all of the above.

The starting point is to establish a clear dashboard for IT. This helps you and the organization establish what good looks like. It sounds obvious, but many IT organizations are run project by project rather than being managed by the business outcome. This stems from the engineering nature of this function.

I always use a set of simple IT ratios to guide me:

Cost

Evaluate the following:

- IT as a percentage of turnover. Here, you need to make sure that you capture all IT costs. Too often, departments have their own 'shadow

(Continued)

IT' budgets, which are used with outside suppliers. Your finance team has to ring-fence the expenditure and stop these additional spend categories.

- IT maintenance costs vs development costs. This gives you an indication of how much money you spend on maintaining your old infrastructure versus the development of new things for the business.

- IT's total cash expenditure across OPEX and CAPEX.

- IT outsource spend. A lot of IT organizations use a multitude of contractors and partners to provide information technology to the business. It is really important to have a reliable overview of the total number of full-time equivalents working inside and outside the business. It is often a myth that you are more efficient and cost effective with outsourcers and contractors.

Reliability

Investigate these key questions:

- What are the number of serious IT incidents per month?

- How many business hours are lost by IT incidents? This gives you an understanding of the real impact of incidents and the time of recovery. It helps to sometimes highlight this by area, such as sales or customer services, because a lost business hour in the back office may have less of a negative impact than an hour where no customer can transact with you.

- What are the existing change windows and planned down time? The more windows you allow, the more potential outages you may trigger.

Time to market of new functionality

Ask yourself:

- How much time is required for the IT organization to deliver new product functionality through new software releases?

- How many times does the IT organization deliver in time, over time or before the forecasted delivery date? Predictability is key because new product launches need more than just IT. They need an ad campaign, sales training, the supply chain, etc.

Once you have a clear understanding of your IT challenge – which includes where you are today and where you need to be in terms of benchmarks – transformation becomes more manageable.

In order to establish the right actions across our IT organization and secure more reliability, we split up the environment into five distinct categories. If your business is suffering from IT instability, this model might be useful for you:

1 Change management

Here, you will have to analyse and improve the existing change management processes across the company. You need to set them up for success. You need to ensure maximum control over change, and excellent alignment and handover between IT and the departments they serve (and for IT to translate these requirements into credible IT changes).

The most expensive IT departments are those that allow too many uncontrolled business change requests. The most expensive I ever managed reported into the chief marketing officer! The creative marketing team would reinvent new IT projects every day, and these changes would lead to outages. Most outages are not created because of bad old systems, but because of changes to existing systems. The most reliable IT environments in the world (such as air traffic control and stock exchange systems) have change windows of just a couple of hours per year.

2 Incident management process

You have to make sure that you have a proper capability to be alerted to all potential incidents in your IT architecture, as well as the tools to manage a fast recovery. You will most likely be surprised by how many IT issues typically come up through your organization and back into IT that you would expect to have been managed and controlled by IT from the start. Unfortunately, we became aware of many IT issues only when customers told us via social media. That is awful. You want IT systems telling your IT people that they're in trouble before a customer is affected.

3 Pro-active health management systems and processes

Often systems become unstable and expensive when they are not checked regularly. Active management of all elements in your IT environment is essential to secure a healthy IT portfolio. It also avoids costly one-off capacity and reliability improvements.

4 Disaster recovery and replication systems and processes

Like an airplane, an IT architecture needs to have in-built recovery and replication capability. Your business needs to continue when one server system is down, or when an entire data centre is affected by a flood, a fire or a major virus attack. However, a disaster recovery and planning model will affect your IT from a cost, reliability and change management perspective. For example, some companies wish to be prepared for that potential flood or fire by installing at least two up-to-date and essentially identical data centres far away from each other. On paper, this makes perfect sense but the implementation and maintenance will drive up IT cost and complexity. In fact, if you do not plan it properly, your reliability may initially suffer as well. In our company, we had firewalls everywhere to prevent hacks. Even between the various IT centres inside my company, there were firewalls. Guess what – the firewall servers often created outages and downtime because they were overloaded. In my time as CEO, we had no hacks from the outside – yet we brought our systems down ourselves.

Every organization needs a disaster recovery model but you need to secure and to monitor the right levels across the IT architecture to avoid outages and to keep costs under control.

5 New application development and delivery

For this area, you will need to analyse, understand, clarify and improve the development of new IT projects and processes. It's key to check to what extent the marketeers and business leaders who are creating new ideas actually engage with the IT experts. In most companies, the general business employee does not understand what the IT systems can deliver in terms of functionality. Hence, you end up with a spaghetti of IT as the specifications the IT department need to find do not exist in the standard software. It is essential to ask IT people how they can solve a business or marketing challenge, rather than asking a business leader to define the scope of IT change.

In many ways, your IT capability should drive your product roadmap rather than the other way around. But watch out – this statement won't make you popular with the people who design new products.

In all transparency, we did not fix all the issues. We continued to have big challenges in this area because we did not deploy the right mix between our own IT capability and outsourced IT services. I guess, like many other companies, after years of outsourcing to reduce costs, we had lost some control and know-how over the IT infrastructure and software of our company.

In 2014, this would result in one of the biggest crises we would face, when the engineer of an outsourced partner pulled the wrong data card out of our network and caused the whole thing to crash. Right across the UK, our customers were unable to make calls for the best part of 12 hours. This could not have happened at a worse time, just days after we had launched our new 'Biggest, Fastest, Best' network campaign on billboards and TV.

It is important to really understand which critical IT functions you should keep in house. Having learned my lessons the hard way, the areas I will retain inside the business in the future are:

- IT operations – where you monitor the systems and applications;

- IT engineering – where you keep the brains of your architecture;

- IT management and business support – where you manage the partners and interface with the business.

The ever-evolving network

The EE network itself was something we could be truly proud of. We had ended 2012 with a significant network capability lead over the competition and we'd exceeded our targets, with 4G having rolled out in a total of 18 cities. Typically, users were getting data rates of between 8 and 12 megabits per second (Mbps) – significantly more than the 1–2 Mbps of 3G networks. We had optimized our sites and were looking to move our 4G coverage forward aggressively – from covering 30 per cent of the population to over half. That meant we were rolling out our network at a rate of 2,000 square miles, and adding coverage for 2 million people, every single month.

We continued to push the boundaries of what a network could do, and what the industry expected. We did that because our customers were demanding it through their actions – through the way they were using 4G, which was becoming central to their everyday lives.

Our trend analysis showed that data usage was going to rise by 750 per cent between 2013 and 2016. That's an unprecedented rate of growth in any industry, and required a new way of thinking, a new understanding of our industry's place in the world, and a new acknowledgement of just how essential our industry had become to communities, companies and consumers.

It used to be the so-called geeks that cared about this kind of stuff. Now it was the gardeners, greengrocers and grandmothers. Everyone from every walk of life – and of all ages – was suddenly using connectivity to make their lives better, fuller, richer.

However grandiose it sounds, superfast connectivity was changing the way people lived their lives. And with exponential usage we could not afford to stand still. With the British population's eagerness for technology at an all-time high, the time was right for us to launch the next stage of our network evolution. We looked at what the future held for networks, and what their requirements would be for a data-hungry nation whose digital consumption bore little relation to today's already super-high usage. They'd need much much more.

We began evolving our network to handle unbelievably fast speeds of up to 300 Mbps, meaning that the UK would surpass South Korea as the fastest mobile nation on Earth.

We launched our 300 Mbps network in 'Tech City' – the area of East London that had become home to hundreds of small digital businesses. It was backed by the British Prime Minister David Cameron, who talked of Britain competing in a 'global race' in technology, explaining that 'the most promising opportunities for new jobs and growth lie within a new wave of high-growth, highly innovative digital businesses'.

Mobile technology was well and truly at the top of the national agenda.

By 2014, we had superfast 4G in 200 major towns and cities, with 95 per cent of the population covered. It was the fastest rollout of any technology in the UK, ever.

Plus, we were rolling out the network to thousands of new villages and small towns – especially in rural parts of the UK – that would, for the first time, be able to access superfast broadband of any kind in their area.

We upgraded our network on key travel routes such as the nation's motorways and major rail networks. For weeks, our network team was travelling hundreds of miles around the M25 to make tiny adjustments to our masts in order to ensure we had the best possible coverage around its entire 117-mile length. Given how much time people spend in traffic jams there, we felt it was pretty important to ensure they experienced as few dropped calls as possible!

Not only did our aggressive rollout boost our credibility as a business with government, our customers and our competitors' customers, it also enabled us to innovate with new products beyond our normal range. We introduced new innovations such as in-car 4G Wi-Fi, Connected Cameras, Personal 4G Hotspots, and insanely large data bundles. In 2014, we became the first operator to launch a petabyte data bundle. One petabyte is a quadrillion bytes. If you used that bundle to download MP3 songs, it would take you 2,000 years to listen to them all. Now, I'm a big fan of Bob Dylan, but there's only so much Blonde on Blonde one man can take.

Evolving your core product and always staying one step ahead of the competition is critical. It's the thing you're known for and have built the business on. Not just gaining leadership – but maintaining it – requires planning, focus, resource and a lot of money (we invested £1.4 million *per day* in rolling out and upgrading our network throughout my time at EE). But get it right, and the payback is significant.

This phase in the evolution of the EE telecommunications network taught me that you always need to re-challenge the status quo. You can never become complacent about your existing product differentiation. Organizations tend to take a capability and a competitive edge for granted. They continue to talk about the success and what has been achieved rather than moving on and maintaining focus on what's around the corner.

Taking up the challenge of serving half of Britain

Alongside the continued transformation of our network and IT, another fundamental part of the business that needed change was service.

Back in the glory days of Orange, the company's service was heralded as champion in the market. This was when the company had under 10 million customers and was able to offer a gold standard of service that was economically viable and structurally manageable.

But Orange had grown, T-Mobile had grown. And together as – and with – EE, we were now taking on the challenge of servicing customers of three brands with a total base of over 25 million connections.

Since the start of the joint venture, our service leader and team had done a great job in maintaining Orange and T-Mobile customer service levels in really challenging times.

But with the launch of EE, it had become highly complex and although we had begun to transform our IT stack, the systems were creaking at the seams.

We had already declared in our manifesto at the start of 2012 that we wanted to have the best network and the best service so that our customers trusted us with their digital lives. Hands down, by the end of 2012, we'd delivered on the promise of the network and, knowing what was on our roadmap, our confidence in this area was growing. Service, however, had not moved in the right direction. In fact, with the addition of a third brand, things had become more difficult for us and for some of our customers.

During the summer of 2013, I once again put service at the heart of our plans to drive loyalty and trust with our customers. A year on, and still we had problems.

In fact, one of my worst days in the EE office was 30 May 2014. Which? – a company that analyses and rates websites, shops, products and customer services in various industries – visited our management team. The CEO of this company took an age to unpack his bag and switch on his PC. He then took his time to share with us the Which? results for the first half of 2014 in retail and customer services across our industry. After a long and meandering preamble, he explained to us that we had come last. We knew we had some challenges in this area, but this was a real blow for us, the team who had declared customer service as a number one priority for the last 18 months.

For too long our performance in service – not the service of our network, but the service we offered customers when they had a question or needed help – was one of the biggest frustrations I had during my time at EE. It was a big frustration for some of our customers too.

Fixing the basics in customer services

Following some significant challenges when we launched the company, we had to restructure, re-align and re-boot our service strategy. Now, three years on, as I write these words, our business is finally moving toward the top in service. The total number of calls per customer is down to around three per year – the industry benchmark. Customer satisfaction measured through Net Promoter Score (more of this later) is up, and we have fantastic stores and call centres in the UK, with thousands of employees who are making the difference.

While the vast majority of our customers were being served brilliantly by our agents, a small number had found themselves being dealt with in a way that made them understandably furious and frustrated. I too was furious and frustrated behind the scenes. After all, we're not in the business of making our customers angry. It was clear that, in spite of all the great work we had delivered on our network, for some time we had struggled to get the customer experience in our call centres consistently right first time, every time.

Sometimes this was due to systems, sometimes due to human error, sometimes due to a process problem. Whatever the issue, it is the one area that we took too long to nail. It is a huge and complex challenge to serve over 25 million people day in, day out, and while I can't say we were 100 per cent successful in transforming service, we ultimately made great strides forward and learned many lessons.

Working toward a tough ambition

Our ambition was to become the number one in customer service for our industry.

Like any ambition, you first need to define exactly what it means, because there are many different ways to become 'number one'. You can have the best customer service because nobody needs to use it, as your promise nearly always delivers (like Amazon). You can have the best customer service because you solve the problems quickly and efficiently but charge for it (IBM for instance). You can have the best customer service image because your staff are exceptionally friendly and go the extra mile for every customer (Waitrose would be a good example).

It is important that you establish one version of the 'number one' truth for your company as it's impossible to excel at everything in this space – especially with a company like EE where the product is an organic and constantly evolving beast.

In order to find the best definition, I recommend that you start by defining the challenges you face in customer services. In our case, it was quite simple: too many customer product processes simply did not get closed, and we had a customer service department that was unable to handle the call volumes. This was a double whammy. We had too many unique calls per customer and a high volume of repeat calls, as we were not closing the issues – a scary combination. We received over 74 million calls per year. Things were made worse by our prehistoric IT systems which would fall over frequently, creating even more waiting times on the line.

We decided to focus first on reducing call volumes by developing a company-wide Propensity to Call (or PTC) reduction programme. It was a project that enabled us to truly understand the reasons why our customers were calling, then track back to – and fix – the root causes. You've to go into real detail to solve problems like these. You have to create, understand and track 'reason codes' for each call type before you can make progress beyond the low-hanging fruit.

We managed to implement a tracking mechanism in our centres. This allowed us to go deep into the various reason codes and their relevance in terms of call volumes and customer dissatisfaction.

Lowering PTC was the right strategy for us because it meant that in a world where our products and processes worked, our customers would not need to call us. The lower volumes of calls enabled us to reduce waiting times too. We not only had to reduce the number of calls per customer, but we also had to tackle unnecessary transfers from one agent to another – a process that would delay and frustrate our customers.

You cannot be rated number one in service if the basics are not under control. I told my organization: 'Our customers expect simple, fast, friendly service – in our stores, on the phone and online. They expect everything to work. And that's what we're going to deliver.'

I can assure you that a simple and direct rallying cry like this works better than the 'we try harder' promise in hotels or car rental services. Too many times, a company with a bland promissory statement does not deliver on that promise. Promising something but not delivering on it is the worst. Predictability and trust are key for customers.

Everyone has had the experience of sitting on a phone support line, hearing how important your call is, but with nobody actually picking up that really important call. So, first get the basics under control before communicating a customer promise:

1 Organize the service function by customer segment and by process, but try to avoid too many handoffs between teams
Ideally, your customer segment team should handle 80–90 per cent of all the key customer queries. Certain more specialized process areas can support the segment teams and handle certain customer issues directly, such as deeply technical calls or complicated billing queries.

2 Ensure your people are productive
Make sure you have the right people in the right places doing the right things for your customers. In a call centre environment, you need to get a handle on absenteeism and performance management. At one point we had an absenteeism rate of above 7 per cent. In a team of over 8,000 people, that's a huge loss to your army. You also need to ensure that your people are not always in training and are actually on the phones helping customers. As part of our investigation into our service challenges, my customer services chief uncovered

that over 30 per cent of our people were in buzz sessions or learning about a new product rather than being on the phones. Our shift and training patterns were wrong. We changed that immediately.

3 Stabilize your IT
Make sure that your IT systems do not fall over. If they do, avoid the support centres. The impact here is often catastrophic. During an IT outage, customers who need support cannot be handled. They will call back later and create even bigger traffic jams on the support lines. You end up in a vicious circle with unhappy customers and de-motivated employees.

4 Analyse your procedures
It is essential to analyse the customer processes and product attributes that generate the largest number of repeat calls and drive the highest propensity to call. Re-engineer them, change them or simply remove them. This area is very hard and requires a cross-company virtual team that drives improvements across the board. Some of these processes will need to be changed through IT projects. It is important to commit money and resources to those, despite the high level of capital expense and time required. These projects will force you to make a trade-off between new innovations and projects that simply fix the mistakes of the past. It is quite frustrating to work on these, but it has to be done. Personally, I made the mistake of delaying these in favour of new product innovation. I won't make that mistake again.

5 Create the right balance between offshore and onshore capabilities
I have had very mixed experience with offshore call centres. In transactional work and for variable increases in capacity they can be excellent. For more complex, technical and new product work they are often challenged. At EE, I decided to re-shore 1,000 jobs from the Philippines because we were too reliant on too many low-quality call centres offshore, with employees who used different technologies and had different cultural experiences from our customers in the UK. Clearly, an on-shoring strategy comes with a cost attached (an offshore employee tends to cost 30–40 per cent less than a UK employee). The unitary cost per call went up, but we were able to lower our overall costs by reducing the number of calls a customer would make from an average of eight per year to

just below four. We also strengthened our first call resolution. This enabled us to reduce overall costs while bringing jobs back to the UK. By bringing resources onshore we also enabled closer alignment between management and the front line. This resulted in a better understanding of the customer experience and allowed us to improve our customer satisfaction significantly.

6 Fix all the key issues raised by your front-line call centre employees
The important word here is 'key'. There will be many issues raised – from hairdryers in the toilets to a different kind of sausage in the canteen – but I'm referring to the ones that will increase customer satisfaction. With an army of service agents each speaking with around 50 customers a day, you can use their knowledge and passion to identify the most important things to fix. You cannot leave any stone unturned if you want to be loved by your customers.

7 Develop one knowledge database across all service channels
Customers get frustrated when they receive inconsistent messages from different customer services agents or through different channels. Therefore, it's important to deploy one version of the truth across all customer touchpoints. The same information needs to be up to date and used across all channels and departments, otherwise you create service inconsistency, which is a big driver of customer dissatisfaction.

If you do not have the time or resources to drive all of the above, simply start by reading and analysing the customer complaints that come into your company. The people who complain about your company can point you to the most important customer pain points.

If the basics are under control, you will potentially be able to tick the 'customer satisfaction' box. This is still a long way away from being number one and driving 'customer loyalty', where customers would actively recommend you to their friends, family, and colleagues. You cannot achieve this by just delivering the standard level of service a customer expects. You'd be surprised if a British Airways pilot came out of the cockpit and asked whether you were now a loyal customer just because he had landed the plane safely. Landing the plane is part of the package. Loyalty comes from the extras.

Creating customer loyalty

At EE, we decided to achieve loyalty primarily through a superior customer interface. We believed that the importance of the customer interface, whether that's digital or in person, was absolutely central to how our customers felt about EE, our network and our place in this world of connectivity. The customer interface is the touchpoint that allows people to enter this world of connectivity easily and with confidence.

As in other areas of the business, great management is essential to driving engagement with your agents who are dealing with the customers. If you have a demotivated and disillusioned army on the phones, then good luck! You will have no chance to become number one in customer services. We had a call centre in Plymouth that always came last in terms of performance against the other centres around the country. Things were so bad there that we seriously considered closing it. Many of the staff seemed to see no correlation between their work and the performance and success of the business. The people were fed up and felt isolated from the rest of the business. Instead of closing it, we decided to bring in a top manager from our best call centre in Wales. That person drove an improvement across the board in less than 12 weeks. Our employee Net Promoter Score – essentially how happy our employees are – moved up from below zero to over 30 within six months!

At the other end of the scale to Plymouth was our Merthyr Tydfil centre. This was our highest-performing site in terms of service delivery and employee motivation, and our lowest in terms of sick leave. The people were dedicated, motivated and excellent at their jobs. For some weeks, we set about trying to understand why, but having analysed the data and completed a full assessment of processes and practices, we still couldn't figure out the root cause of why this centre – and its people – were our top performers. It wasn't until the management team and I visited the site and spoke with its people that the penny dropped. At lunch, we sat in the canteen with the employees to share with them our plans for the business and get their thoughts on how we could improve. I was sitting next to one of our call centre agents and asked her the question straight out. Why did she think this was our top-performing centre? 'The thing is', she said, 'here in Merthyr there're only two options when you leave school. Since the Hoover factory closed down a few years back, you can either join the call centre or go to work at the abattoir. We know that if we do well, the business will do well, and the call centre will stay open. If we don't, the call centre may close and then it's off to the abattoir for us.'

Driving motivation and performance requires your employees to have a clear understanding of where the company is going, what it stands for, what it wants to achieve in the market and what part they play in that success. Add in decent team mates who have mutual respect, clarity about compensation, flexible working hours, potential to develop within the business, and a strong respected manager, and you have the recipe for a motivated workforce.

In my experience, it is really hard to create the right winning spirit in call centres that operate with more than 1,000 people. I love to work with medium-sized teams (up to 800) in areas where there is sufficient young talent available, but not where you have to compete with hundreds of other firms for the same talent pool. It is good to have multiple centres in different locations competing with each other and run by strong local management teams. Running local apprentice schemes and charity activities will further strengthen the performance and spirit of the centre.

It is amazing how you can drive motivation for the company if you start creating new jobs for young people. I remember meeting Andrew in our Doxford call centre. He was one of our apprentices. He had worked in a pub for a few years, but when the recession came, the leisure industry was hit hard and the small family hostelry he worked for couldn't keep on their staff. They let him go.

Not long after that, Andrew was living hand to mouth and couldn't afford the rent for his flat. He was evicted, and with no money, he was forced to move into a homeless hostel and was claiming benefits. Having tried – and failed – to get steady work, he went on a sales and services course at his local job centre. While on the course, he was put forward for an apprenticeship with EE.

When Andrew started working for us he moved out of the hostel and into a shared house. Afterwards, he was looking to buy his own house. He told me that, like me, he loves cooking, and couldn't wait to cook in his own kitchen. That would mean that his daughter could come and stay with him at weekends and have her own room. Andrew said that all this was now within reach because the EE apprenticeship scheme had seen his potential and given him a chance.

I found meeting Andrew a truly humbling experience. It was one of the best moments in my career. Transformation can change not just company fortunes, but people's lives too.

The power of the Net Promoter Score tool set

Our overall goal in motivating our employees was to drive up customer loyalty. There are different ways to measure success in this area. We decided to use Net Promoter Score – or NPS – across the organization. The advantage of this measurement is that you can apply it in every area. Also, it's a tough and thorough measure for the business – a very credible way to measure success.

NPS is based on a direct question: How likely is it that you would recommend our company, product or service to a friend or colleague? The scoring for this answer is most often based on a 0–10 scale. Promoters are those who respond with a score of 9 or 10 and are considered loyal enthusiasts. Detractors are those who respond with a score of 0 to 6, unhappy customers. Scores of 7 and 8 are passives, and they will only count towards the total number of respondents, but do not directly affect the formula. NPS is calculated by subtracting the percentage of customers who are Detractors from the percentage of customers who are Promoters.

Companies with a better ratio of Promoters to Detractors tend to grow more rapidly than their competitors. Companies with the most efficient growth engines operate with an NPS of 50 to 80. The average firm splutters along with an NPS of only 5 to 10 – in other words, their Promoters barely outnumber their Detractors. Many firms – and some entire industries – have negative Net Promoter Scores, which means that they are creating more Detractors than Promoters day in, day out. These low scores explain why so many companies can't deliver profitable, sustainable growth no matter how aggressively they spend to acquire new business.

With NPS, each area in the business should have its own targets, linked to employee reward. Because customer services fix problems and the retail stores are selling the product, these processes have very different NPS scores. It is key to understand where each part of your organization sits on their respective scale. If you know what the status quo is, you can then set the targets for improvement.

We got it wrong the first time and created a lot of dissatisfaction among our people as bonuses were negatively impacted – even for those teams that made great progress. That said, you have to build NPS into the compensation of your front-line teams, otherwise you simply don't get the traction required. When we got it right, it worked a treat, with our people incentivized to ensure our customers were happy.

Customer services cannot be fixed in isolation. It requires an end-to-end analysis, planning, and a clear game plan. It is seriously hard because it often challenges other priorities like bringing in innovation, cost management, and revenue optimization.

Three years on, we're still working on creating a number one service organization at EE. It is an astonishingly tough task when you're dealing with legacy systems, a huge base of employees and customers, and a rapidly changing industry that never stays still.

Perhaps you've experienced similar challenges in your business, where important transformation drives IT change, often leading to business interruptions, cost overruns, and delays. Your employees and customers often suffer as a result. IT and customer services tend to be the hardest and most difficult areas to fix and control, as every person, every process, and every product in your company directly impacts the customer. Small mistakes from the past can be tough to identify and unravel, and every decision taken yesterday, today and tomorrow will have ramifications and knock-on effects in some other part of the business.

My learning is to go 'deep and broad' in your personal understanding and involvement in these areas. Understand every system, every impact and every root cause, using top leaders who are equally fixated with every detail of the process.

Most importantly, understand and learn from your people on the front line. They generally have the answers.

In most industries, including telecoms and banking, customer services is labelled a cost centre. That makes it much harder to transform than in industries where people get charged for service, such as IT sectors. Try and adjust your own and your business's thinking about this.

Supercharging sales

09

I have never worked a day in my life without selling. If I believe in something, I sell it, and I sell it hard.
ESTÉE LAUDER

> At the heart of every business is a transaction – a transaction between the organization and its customer. Because of that, pretty much every company has a sales function (unless there is no competition, such as with some government services or a unique monopoly).
>
> So isn't it strange that, unlike finance, PR, marketing or engineering, there are very few – if any – higher education courses that focus on sales?
>
> In this chapter, I'll be sharing my lessons in sales with you – specifically on how to transform and move a sales function forward. Essentially, I will cover how go-to-market models in retail, in digital, and in business-to-business can become high-performance areas in your company.

Breaking records with 4G

The real success of a business transformation will be shown through the numbers. After all of the complexities, obscurities and mysteries of business, the numbers tell it like it is. Your actions have either been successful, or they have failed.

With EE, we set out to deliver the most successful 4G rollout and adoption not just in the UK, but globally. Many people said we would fail. In fact, we ended up beating all records for adoption of 4G in Europe.

By the end of 2013, over a million UK people and businesses had turned on to 4G. We had now sold over 100 superfast 4G contracts every hour of every day since launch.

It was astonishing progress that would continue throughout the following year. By the end of 2014 we had exceeded 7 million 4G customers.

We now had more customers taking 4G contracts than 3G contracts. And for the first time, more data was being used on EE's 4G plans than on the older, more established brands of Orange and T-Mobile. In fact, 4G data usage per customer was up 66 per cent compared to the start of the year.

As I write this in early 2016, we have reached 15 million 4G customers. An incredible result.

It was a step change for our business. But it didn't happen just because we had set the imaginations of the UK alight with a service that changed the way they could access whatever they wanted, wherever they were.

It happened because we had also set about transforming our sales function which, like its peers in the industry, had not seen significant change since the last century.

There are not many books written about sales transformation or how to create a high-performance sales organization. There is not a university degree in sales, and apart from some *Harvard Business Review* articles, few academics have done in-depth research regarding sales. I have always wondered why such an important area of business hasn't caught the same academic imagination as marketing, finance, manufacturing, or the supply chain. HP's Mark Hurd once told me that the only key people inside a technology company are sales people and engineers. Everyone else is an overhead!

I have always focused on sales – especially the front line, because the rubber hits the road with these people. Stuff gets done and I enjoy being among them. They are mostly independent, un-political, driven and optimistic – the good ones at least. However, transformation of sales is challenging because there are a lot of people and a lot of different sales channels.

Transforming a business-to-consumer function

The transformation of a business-to-consumer (B2C) sales organization is fundamentally different to the transformation of a business-to-business (B2B) one. You cannot apply the same techniques.

The starting point is to define your B2C existing routes to market – web, telesales, retail, indirect channels, direct sales and so on. You should map these against the market. Are there gaps? Do you have enough retail stores to cover the geography? Do you have a fit-for-purpose web store? Do you have enough (or too many) indirect partners? Do you have a telesales organization? The initial work in these areas is straightforward, but will only tell you the full story when you have unitary cost information versus key benchmarks and productivity data. Unitary cost information looks at the fully loaded cost of one sales entity.

For example, the unitary cost of one retail store concept is built around how many people work there, the rent, the light bulbs, the furniture, and so on. You then map this information against sales numbers. This gives you a granular overview of the gap between that channel and the total market potential, as well as productivity versus a benchmarked unitary cost model. This data enables you to start defining the strengths, weaknesses, opportunities and threats of your sales model. Based on this information you can begin articulating a desired end-state sales model defined by the mix between the routes to market (for example, how much do you want to sell through retail versus the web). It will also enable you to benchmark your sales productivity ratios by channel as well as the necessary optimization in terms of unitary cost.

When we did this analysis inside EE it told us that we fell short on every level. Because of the joint venture, we had over 700 stores – more than any other mobile operator. Worse than that, they were often on exactly the same high street and sometimes literally next door to each other – one for Orange and one for T-Mobile. They were also not particularly productive. In 2012, a Vodafone store would typically do 80 per cent more transactions than us. Fifty per cent of our sales were dependent on expensive indirect partners, whereas the figure for the rest of the market was around 40 per cent. In telesales and web, we were even further behind the competition.

In addition to problems in channel mix and volume productivity, the sales model was entirely driven by volume, not by value. This resulted in enormous wastage. Expensive sales channels like retail would focus on the least valuable products to hit their volume targets. The value was further compromised by attacks by fraudsters. Through identity fraud, crooks were able to get access to free mobile phones by signing a contract but never paying. Fraud reached over 20 per cent of sales in certain product categories.

We had to take a deep breath before changing everything – there was a lot to do.

We established three simple priorities – getting the right people, driving better value, and growing our direct channels. We established a desired end state and began our delivery of this by changing the top people in our sales organization. We changed the entire sales leadership team (except telesales, which had solid management but not enough focus and resource). We focused on hiring the best leaders in each area. We were able to secure top leaders for retail, indirect channels, and the web.

Retail transformation

The most rewarding days in my job are when I visit store staff who don't know I'm coming. The experience is fantastic. The staff are professional and positive, the stores look good, they are clean, our customers seem happy and the demos work. The basics, but success from where we had come from – and it wasn't easy to get there. Only now, at the beginning of 2016, is our main retail channel transformation successfully completed.

To transform retail for success, I recommend applying a few simple tricks.

In order to secure the right store footprint, make sure that your sales leadership team drives analysis and decision making based on store unitary cost, productivity and market-relevant information such as potential, existing and future customer density, demographics, and competitive stores. Before you close a store, make sure you really understand the true potential of it. You'll find, to your cost, that it's much easier and quicker to close one of your stores than to build a new one.

After you have developed a store footprint focus, and once you have hired the best retail leader you can find, focus on your people.

The right shops and the right people

The hardest and most important part of transforming a retail estate is the people. You have to hire, retain, train, and motivate this organization to become the best. Your transformation starts with the store managers. In order to create passion with that organization, you need to prioritize their focus onto brand-building activities, training and communication. They need to feel that they are the true customer interface of the company and that they are supported accordingly.

As with every part of the business, it's your people who will make or break your transformation. In retail, this is even more pronounced as they represent your company to the customer, every single day. They are the face of your brand, more important than a smart logo, and with more potential to make – or break – your business, depending on their performance, knowledge and behaviours. Assess their performance. Let them know that you only want the best shop managers to work in your company and be really clear about what you mean by the best. Then drive performance improvement from top to bottom. Leaders are sometimes hesitant to be frank and open about performance management within organizations, but I can assure you that sales managers and sales people want you to be as direct about their performance as possible. They can handle tough and clear language and are often more remote from – and more hardened than – the general employee population. It is essential to explain performance in their language and not in some corporate blurb.

If you start proper performance management of shop managers, you will improve productivity and customer satisfaction quickly.

The performance expectation and aspired sales behaviour need to be 100 per cent aligned to their sales compensation – otherwise, your motivation model will not be seen as credible.

Often, I've found that compensation schemes are not in line with what you would expect as the CEO. Many times the sales compensation model is more a reflection of the organizational hierarchy of its business areas, rather than driving the right sales behaviour with customers and the maximization of sales potential. Check it yourself. Go into a store and understand the exact measurement of the manager and his employees before you go onstage at your first retail sales kick-off event. The CEO has to understand this level of detail.

The science of sales compensation

The challenge of sales compensation for a store is that the shop manager typically needs a different scorecard from his or her sales team. Our store managers were measured on a total number of successful commercial acts by business area (eg mobile, broadband, additional services). Each of these business areas was gated in the compensation to make sure that the shop achieved each individual business target. This gating system does not apply to the sales people working for the shop manager as it is too hard to measure every individual on every business area. Value improvement is secured by accelerators that focus on upsell and product mix. Individual sales people have a clear bonus system defined by each type of sale.

Overall, it should all fit nicely on a whiteboard at the back of the retail store. My rule of thumb is if the store manager cannot write the entire compensation and measurement model for his team on that board, it is too complex.

In other businesses, I have delegated the P&L all the way to the front-line manager. In my experience this can be very effective – assuming you can focus the people on the right drivers of a P&L. If every shop manager focuses on the best-value product because it drives the best P&L but is in short supply, you drive the wrong result. It is hard to keep a P&L-based compensation system in line with the real dynamic movements of P&L drivers. That's why, over time, I have moved away from it as a model.

I have worked with partners who transitioned from individual variable compensation of the front line to a team-based model to secure the best customer experience. Their belief is that it avoids mis-selling and focuses on the best deal for the customer. In my view, this has the massive disadvantage that you may end up with the sales road of least resistance – a low price.

Here are my key principles when building the reward incentives for a retail team:

- Keep it simple.
- Include at least one credible, measurable customer satisfaction KPI (Net Promoter or Customer Satisfaction scores).
- Translate top trading objectives into clear unitary goals.
- Secure value focus by driving the right mix and upsell targets.
- Make sure that each individual can influence at least 90 per cent of their measured objectives – the compensation system needs to reward top performance and drive people to go the extra mile.
- Keep it consistent over a period of time – don't change it every three months.

Retail is detail

The second trick to transform retail successfully is to apply the rule that 'retail equals detail'. It means that every little detail in a store counts. I expect our store managers to treat their store like the most important room in their own home. It has to be super clean, beautiful, posters hung straight, with demo equipment that works, sufficient inventory and working digital screens. If there is a quiet moment in the store, the store staff should work on the look and the feel. 'Retail equals detail' also means that there needs to be a very high level of consistency across your store estate and that the sales journey in a store needs to be optimized and meticulously planned dependent on the different store formats.

As with customer services (see previous chapter), the consistency in the buying experience across different stores and different routes to market is key. We decided to drive one consistent sales process – from welcoming the customer to closing the deal – using one information database across all stores. The leadership team of EE spent hours in mock-up stores testing new products, processes, and messaging before it went live across an entire estate. We decided early on to create a detailed test retail environment to try out new stuff and train sales staff.

To date, I have visited hundreds of our 600 retail stores, many stores of the competition, and best-in-class stores from other industries. When I visited EE stores, I'd make sure that no one knew I was coming – that way I got to see the reality of the working environment. I love to be with our front-line people in the stores. They tell me everything – what works, what doesn't. I listen and observe, keeping a simple log of the good, the bad and the average. I rated every store I visited, and provided feedback to my chief sales officer and his retail director.

Digital transformation

With customer behaviours transitioning from the physical to the virtual worlds, digital sales and marketing channels have gained huge importance in nearly every business over the past few years. Typically, it's the area that is hardest to develop and change because the underlying systems are old and out of date. It's also expensive to change because older digital sales and marketing systems were built around business processes in your company that are not suited to your current customers or the current business model. To begin transforming this area, you will have to start by reviewing, mapping, and improving the actual business processes that are the foundation for your digital environment. This is painful and takes a lot of time. The good news is that you will find an enormous amount of off-the-shelf modern IT and software tools that have been designed specifically for your industry and your type of business. Unless you need your digital channel to be a unique and strategic asset – something that operates in a way that is markedly different to your competitors – you can save time and money by amending your processes to the ones that were used to design the standard package. If your plan requires you to change more than 30 per cent of the code of the software your digital team wants to use, I suggest you search for another package or challenge your business processes.

Your leaders in this area are key. The professionalization of the digital industry is one of the most recent developments in business organizations. You will typically find four types of leaders in this world:

- **The web techie** – the IT manager who was responsible for web stuff in the IT back room and has been promoted to e-commerce leader (often because of in-depth knowledge of systems).

- **The web marketer** – who grew up in web design, look and feel, and has been promoted to be the boss of all things digital (because he can make the customer experience look and function beautifully).

- **The web entrepreneur** – who launched a small .com company that did well but didn't IPO, so he now finds himself in a corporate role (and often brings maverick behaviour to your process-driven corporate world – sometimes welcomed, sometimes not).

- **The traditional product business leader** – who always wanted to get into a 'new world' (and brings new thinking, but not a huge amount of technical knowledge).

If digital plays a major part in your sales, marketing and services strategy, pick a strong business leader who may have had extensive experience in this world, but who definitely has the skills to translate that into the language of a more traditional, non-digital company. Empower this person by giving them authority over all external digital spend – the money your company spends with web agencies, web consultants, and so on. If you have the right leader you will save some money by avoiding shadow web design and shadow IT.

I also recommend that you allow your digital leader to in-source key software engineers, web developers, web designers and project management talent. The digital area is becoming increasingly relevant in your industry, like in mine, so it is important to make your company more digitally savvy, more attractive for digital experts, and less reliant on agencies that work for both you and your competitors.

Personally, I like to keep IT strategy, infrastructure, and tools in one dedicated IT organization. The digital team will focus on all e-commerce sites, the e-service sites, and your website internally and externally. They are measured on business results from these four categories and drive change across all of them. You have to avoid managing them by 'features'. All too often I have seen a digital team proudly present all the new gadgets – rolling icons, new search capabilities and fancy new colours – while your customers are not growing their spend online and are still calling your service centres instead of using the online e-service tools.

If your team tells you that they have to change the digital environment with new tools, millions of pounds and a lot of time, consider the following:

- As we have already ascertained, the average shelf life of a CEO is around three to four years. Consequently, your digital team will have to deliver the cost and revenue benefits of their plan within the first 24 months. Ideally, you should give them only 12 months. Otherwise, it's no use to you. For some strange reason, you and your business operation always have to deliver quarter after quarter, while IT and digital teams typically think in years! If you allow them to have a three-year programme, the scope and requirements will probably change three or four times, the costs will go up and you will potentially never get to see the benefits. If there is no choice because of the overarching complexity of the existing digital systems, at least break it up into annual deliveries that have tangible business benefits along the way.

- New systems and tools must deliver against strict business requirements rather than vague functional time-to-market benefits. Every bit of software you buy in a shop will promise you those things. Your digital team has to commit to achieving real profit and cash improvements from the new stuff. Otherwise, they may succeed, but you will still have your miserable quarters to deal with.

- Allow the digital team to define what needs to be done in alignment with the rest of the company. If you let the rest of the company define what digital has to deliver, you will end up with just another version of the spaghetti system you already have! I am a big believer that IT and digital define business process rather than the other way around. Once, in a previous e-commerce-based job, I tried to accommodate all of my colleagues. It ended up as a big mess of digital features and processes. We changed it by looking at the customer view, delivering best practices, and ensuring business alignment. It was ultimately a success because the rest of the business bought into our intended results and metrics. They signed those off, and afterwards the digital team was empowered to put it in place and deliver.

- It is important to bring the IT roadmap and priorities back to the leadership team of the company on a regular basis to ensure that the digital team can execute the most important projects for the business. As almost every new business idea requires an IT implementation, the roadmap will always get clogged up unless the leadership team reviews and signs it off on a regular basis.

Now, once you have completed all of this, always remember that your retail stores, your website, and the front line engagement with customers will define your company. That's why I decided that for EE, those three areas are always leading in terms of branding and overall communication. They are constantly representing the company to the outside world.

The multi-channel future

So far, I have shared some ideas about retail, call centres and digital routes to market.

It's important to look at all of these channels because today's customers inform themselves, decide, and purchase across a range of different media. In the past, people would have been comfortable researching and booking a vacation package tour with a travel agent or over the phone. Now, the majority of people will use every channel available to them throughout the purchasing cycle. Clearly, the digital channel via mobile is gaining huge importance, but in the end, both the physical and the digital channels have merit and must be invested in – both in terms of your time and your business's money. Just as traditional 'physical' businesses are understanding the importance of the digital channel, so the 'digital' businesses are understanding the importance of the 'physical' channel. This is no better exemplified than by the fact that Amazon is planning to open high street stores.

The future's best-in-class companies have the following attributes:

- They have the best seamless customer experience across various routes to market. This multi-channel experience requires complete alignment and always up-to-date sales and service information across digital, retail and call centre teams.

- They have differentiated themselves through additional multi-channel functionality and intelligent customer-centric services like 'click and collect' and 'click to chat'.

- They have multi-channel customer data analysis, which provides insights into where and how customers interact with the company. These insights can identify negative experience points and positive triggers to drive customers to transact.

Transforming a business-to-business function

I have managed several business-to-business (B2B) sales forces during my career.

One of the most exciting moments in my career was to present to over 5,000 B2B sales people and managers at a conference in Disneyland near Paris during the annual sales kick-off of HP.

I had the graveyard slot at the end of the day – a 45-minute closing pitch to people who had been listening for hours and just wanted to go home. Everyone was tired of partying in Disneyland and listening to the roll call of company speakers. There's only so much Mickey Mouse any self-respecting business person can take!

Great B2B sales people are numbers-driven, confident (but not arrogant), disciplined, self-motivated, extrovert and charismatic – that's why it's really hard to present to them! But it was exhilarating to stand in front a team that was now truly motivated and successful.

We were winning big businesses across Europe against IBM. There was a new sales management system in place, a different sales model, and real energy and confidence. We had completed a long and hard transformation of the B2B corporate account sales force.

The honest assessment of a B2B sales force

We had started by talking to the top CIOs in Europe, the Middle East and Africa to collect qualitative feedback about our sales force. Why did we not win big projects? Why did they rate our account management below IBM? We also looked at quantitative data from customers. It didn't give us much more new information, but would help convince our sales organization to transform. If your customers tell your sales people to change, they're more likely to do it.

The transformation centered on people, processes, skills, models, measurement and compensation.

B2B sales is fundamentally a people-to-people game. The people side has to be right. Most companies focus on performance management and skills training. I focused on performance management and skills assessment. We decided not to treat our people like school kids, but simply to hold a mirror up to them and show them where they were versus our company expectations. Each individual had to do a self-assessment against our ideal profile. Afterwards, they would see how their manager rated them against the same profile. Together, they formed the basis for a skills gap analysis and an overview for us. The sales people had six months to fill the gaps. For a lot of people it was a real eye-opener to understand the skill requirements and the mismatch between their own view about their capabilities and that of their manager. This system is designed to develop motivation – which it will do unless the person is a non-performer. We made a mistake of undertaking this fairly expensive self-assessment with all employees. The next time I used the same concept I deployed it after a performance management sweep through the company. This was way more effective as we used the 'mirror technique' only on the people we wanted to retain in the company.

As part of the assessment, we created an assessment board made up of senior leaders from the business. They reviewed the performance improvements six months after the self-assessment. As part of that review, the sales leader had to participate in a thorough sales presentation model. We played the part of the board of a company, listening to the sales pitch of the account manager. It was a real pressure-cooker environment for the account managers and gave them an opportunity to sharpen their solution sales skills.

It's hard to drive improvements across a very large B2B sales force. My trick to accelerate change started with the selection of a strong top team followed by building a direct communication link to the first-line management. Instead of cascading messaging throughout the entire hierarchy – which had five management layers – I decided to shorten the communication and focus the attention on the last, or as I see it, first line of management.

The combination of strong performance management, hiring the best top sales leaders, the skills assessment, and driving communication to first-line management was essential to start the transformation.

In parallel, we began addressing the critical *processes*. There was not even a generally accepted standard in the major account sales process. Sales was seen as an art and not a science, which was crazy. So many companies believe great sales is only about the salesperson themselves – that you have to hire and pay for this amazing account-buster, the 'born salesman' with the killer instinct. Due to their maverick nature, this often perpetuates the belief that there's no need for a disciplined sales process. 'Don't worry', you'll be told, 'they'll get you the deal'. This is, of course, nonsense. Sales is not an art but depends on structure, planning, process, metrics and people.

A five-step sales process to deliver

At EE, we decided to use a really simple five-step sales process: Qualification, Offer, Negotiation, Close, Grow.

We built a standardized funnel management system and reporting processes using Siebel systems. This replaced the existing numerous unreliable systems we had historically operated. After a painful nine-month IT process redesign and implementation, we had one unique version of the truth. I made sure that any deal that was not tracked in the funnel management system would not be taken into account in compensating management or the individual account managers. In the beginning, there were quite a few unhappy campers. The long-tenure 'sales artists' were masters in trying to hide deals until late in the process in order to avoid over-ambitious targets. Most deals had nine- to twelve-month sales cycles, so would be visible in the budgeting phase. However, 'no compensation' was a pretty simple and effective tool to get all deals into our cockpit.

The information helped us to start managing the pipeline and our individual account managers. Some account managers were brilliant in shaping deals but terrible in going through the five-step process in a reasonable amount of time. Bad velocity can cost the company far too much. This five-step process helps to manage deal size, win rate, velocity, and the overall pipeline.

At EE, we centred on four other critical processes to win in B2B:

- **Major account planning process**

  Here the key is to create an account business plan. It is typically an annual process whereby the lead account manager creates visibility of the opportunities, existing business, a relationship matrix, costs and ideally an account P&L overview. The best account plan process I have used was called a 'carousel' process whereby the account manager agreed with every product area, developed an individual plan to secure a maximum set of opportunities, and agreed investments. The bigger the account, the longer the carousel can take.

- **Annual account coverage review process**

  During this process, you try to identify if your B2B account manager is force-covering the end-customer companies in your market. This is important because you need to understand, at least annually, if your organization is missing out on important new businesses, or on the right ones, depending on their evolution and willingness to consider working with your company. Account prioritization and selection is crucial. I will never

(Continued)

forget, earlier on in my career, trying to win one of the largest desktop outsourcing contracts in Europe based on just a conversation with the CIO and his team. We spent one year with 30 people trying to win the business. We won the deal, popped the champagne and, hey presto, the CEO decided a few days later to cancel the project altogether. It was too risky. He told me afterwards, 'I was never a fan of this one.' A huge amount of wasted time and money could have been avoided through a more rigorous account review process.

- **Account satisfaction process**
  Here, there are many standard processes available (such as eRAP or NPS). Pick one as your standard, but never rely on the surveys alone. Stay close and engage directly with the most important accounts.

- **Executive sponsorship and lighthouse account process**
  In my experience, you will find it tough to win any big deals from the competition unless there are strong relationships in place between the most senior executives in your company and the customer. These relationships need to be built and nurtured. They take time. Unfortunately, not everyone in your team will like being a sales person – many love to review account managers but not support them. Therefore, you will need to force a process that establishes relationship targets inside the top accounts that are mapped against the top people in your organization. A simple briefing and reporting process would accompany this. I normally link this process with an identification of must-wins and major 'lighthouse' accounts from the competition – the icons in the market. If they are choosing to work with your company, they will shine a light on the rest of the market.

We had huge success at EE using these tried-and-tested methods. We moved from being simply not considered against the likes of Vodafone – the operator with the largest B2B heritage – to swiping some of their biggest customers from under their noses. It was a lot of fun – for us, at least.

The small business sector required less major transformation at EE, as Orange and T-Mobile were traditionally strong in this area. However, the key to success in this market is a committed indirect partner network, combined with dedicated customer services and a standardized product portfolio to ensure consistency, profitability and serviceability.

During 2015, we ended up with double-digit growth in the corporate account segment as huge British and multinational companies flocked to EE looking for its superfast network to supercharge their business. This also helped us to further strengthen our position in the small and medium segment – a small business would have more confidence buying from us when big accounts like Sky, Deloitte and Fujitsu put their trust in EE as well.

Don't you think it would be easier if you could hire sales leaders for digital, retail, B2B, and telesales, who have had a specific education in this area? You wouldn't hire an engineer who does not have an engineering degree, nor a CFO without an accountancy or financial education.

Sales is the engine of your business and yet, without any real sales university or qualification, you mostly rely on 'experience' for hiring talent.

If you want the best sales engine in your industry, you have to find the best sales management who can create high-performance routes to market through rigorous unitary cost management, process management, multi-channel alignment, and, obviously, people selection, assessment, development, compensation and retention.

Sales is a science, not an art.

The £12.5 billion business 10

The biggest inhibitor of corporate innovation is a focus on the short-term financial results... In most universities, MBA students will learn how to do 'zero-based budgeting' and not 'how to innovate'.
SIR MARTIN SORRELL, SPEAKING AT THE FOUNDERS FORUM 2015

The penultimate chapter of this book focuses on the financial transformation of a business, which is the result of everything you have read so far. We'll look at where to begin, how cash is king, suppliers – and getting those relationships and deals right is key – and how to drive real profitability within your business.

Ultimately, the numbers show your success, but there are some key decisions and leaps of faith that need to be taken early on to ensure success in the long term.

In this chapter we also look at how we took a disillusioned organization and turned it into one that delivered from the ground up.

Kick-starting a financial transformation

At EE, we drove our overall profitability from a low EBITDA of 18 per cent to a market-leading 28 per cent in just four years. This was an amazing result.

The business transformation I have described in this book ultimately delivered an enterprise value swing from £8.5 billion to over £12.5 billion. This was only possible because we transformed our financials fundamentally and were able to generate more profit and cash – but it was also based on a new multiple. If you turn the number three and four players into a clear industrial leader with a sustainable network and clear service differentiation, you are worth more to your existing – and new – shareholders. Business transformation has made your company more sustainable, more profitable, and more exciting. That's the aim of the game.

But doing it is not easy, and you will not be able to achieve the financial objectives you have promised to your shareholders unless you are able to express business transformation in a detailed financial map that transforms the P&L and the balance sheet of the company positively.

At EE, fortunately, our balance sheet was very healthy. We did not need to start a financial rescue plan before transforming into an industry leader. Our debt levels were below those of our competitors and we were generating cash, albeit at a low percentage of revenue. Consequently, our excellent CFO could even start a corporate bond programme to further strengthen our financial capacity.

So we started at the most obvious place – by trying to understand the operational financial P&L state of our business compared to our peers and the benchmarks. Having done that, we established two plans – one plan for our shareholders and one for ourselves.

Our shareholder plan ensured (at a minimum) the delivery of underlying profitability expressed in a percentage as well as in pound notes. It is imperative that you deliver your shareholders a reasonable plan that has a high chance of success. You do not win points by missing financial goals. In fact, doing so will damage your ability to raise money with bondholders or shareholders to support the transformations you need to make. You will probably lose your job as well. If you are not predictable about the bottom line (cash and profitability) to the people who loan – and trust you with – the money, you do not deserve more.

Your second plan is your internal plan, which needs to be flexible from a cost management perspective and (potentially) from a revenue perspective. The cost side is key. Nobody can accurately plan revenue, because there are factors that are hard to predict, such as your competitors' actions and new regulations. But every business can at least plan how it spends on the absolute necessities, and on driving unitary costs that are aligned to the benchmarks in your industry.

The importance of cash management

Clearly, large or small companies require decent cash generation. Cash is king and ultimately pays the bills.

Solid cash management will require exceptionally tight management processes around your CAPEX and cost centres. It is striking how many managers in your business will spend hours at home considering different travel operators and websites to buy their £2,000 family vacation, but sign off purchase orders for millions of pounds without even blinking.

It is quite hard to establish cash-generating key performance indicators across the entire organization. If you can clearly link the individual work objectives with a cash objective, it is good to do so. Otherwise, use the key drivers – revenue, margin, OPEX, CAPEX – to develop a solid plan.

The one department that has to be 100 per cent focused on cash generation is the finance function. They have to be your cash control workhorse, day in and day out.

The first key requirement to help keep cash under control is to generate lots of revenue. Easier said than done. Forecasting and planning revenue is hard. Competition, regulatory effects, currency developments, economic cycles, disruptive technologies and many other factors make revenue more unpredictable than what you spend.

That's why good business leadership starts by understanding and managing unitary costs. As we have covered previously in this book, most companies in the same industry have similar ideas. It is all about execution, and driving better time to market and resource management. Unitary costs help you to understand the underlying cost drivers of your product and process. De-layering unitary costs, reinventing ways of delivering the same objective at a lower unitary cost, and constantly benchmarking this area, are crucial tools to help in managing costs.

At EE, we frequently ran a Business Transformation Programme (BTP), which challenged the underlying cost drivers of the business and improved them through project management. One of the ideas we executed within BTP was an outsourcing/insourcing model.

EE is a UK-only business. Therefore, we could not complete significant labour arbitration (which is the ability to take advantage of lower labour costs) without working with traditional outsourcers (Infosys, Tony Harris, IBM, and so on). I do not like these models because it is very hard to integrate these suppliers into your company's culture and environment. Plus, you don't want to hand off your key assets and processes. So, instead, we decided to develop our own 'in-house outsourced centre' in Chisinau, Moldova. The employees there would work only for EE, under our control but facilitated by a local telecom operator. This model helped us to keep critical capability in house while reducing our unitary costs in a number of areas.

The front line can play a key role here as well. I have seen brilliant examples of the simple employee 'idea box', where employees can submit cost efficiency ideas in and around their function. If the idea is selected by the BTP team, the employee participates in detailed solution development and implementation. More than any award they would receive, many employees – especially in the front line – were hugely excited about effecting change in the organization and having their chance to play with a bit of the train set.

The key to supplier management

Clearly, keeping a key handle on your costs also comes from tight management of your suppliers and through a rigorous purchasing management system. When I joined EE, we had way too many suppliers. Each area had their own preferred supplier ranging from contractors and digital agencies to large network equipment suppliers. Right at the start of the EE transformation, we began to tighten this up, reducing the number of key suppliers significantly. It enabled us to negotiate larger spend categories with fewer suppliers and ultimately allowed us to save millions.

I am a big believer on bundling spend. A few months before I joined the business, I even introduced the concept of sharing spend across our two massive worldwide operators – our shareholders France

Telecom and Deutsche Telekom. We created a purchasing joint venture between the two companies that had the objective to save €1.3 billion annually. We brought home this huge saving in three ways. First, we picked the best of two contracts across several categories. Second, we unlocked large-volume purchasing and economies of scale. And finally, we developed new lower-cost industrial standards and best-in-class purchasing processes (learning lessons from other industries such as the 'Just In Time' model from the car industry). Clearly, there are strict regulatory rules around this – we certainly stayed far away from the critical market share level (which sits at around 15 per cent globally).

These projects fail unless you can truly control local buying. If you simply develop and sign a framework agreement with suppliers and leave separate local negotiations in place, it does not work. Employees love to work with their favourite suppliers and manage purchasing themselves. Signing a PO equals power for the individual, but can mean wastage for the business as a whole. If you can develop an integrated purchasing process which pulls together strong targeted local buying with over-arching large-volume purchasing through head office, you win.

At the end of the day, superior cost management comes from a management culture to be 'stingy' – like a Dutchman – and cost-aware at all times.

Driving revenue profitably

Aside from cost management, profitable revenue is the essential ingredient for your cash flow generation.

The transformation of EE has taught me that a quality business attracts quality customers – and quality customers have a positive impact on margin. The revenue can be pretty much the same but if it is generated by a different customer mix, it can become significantly more profitable. For example, the adjusted EBITDA of EE grew to over 28 per cent during 2015 with no revenue growth. We had a double-digit year-on-year improvement because our business model had improved. Among other things, that was thanks to a growth in business customers, in contract consumer customers, and, overall, in

4G customers. Bad debt levels improved. Customers paid their bills more quickly. Margin and cash improved.

Smart pricing management

Most businesses spend a decent amount of time on marketing the hell out of their broad range of products and services in order to generate more revenue. However, there are fantastic digital tools available nowadays to analyse existing pricing, predict price elasticity, enable yield price management and recommend price strategies. I bundle these under the 'smart' pricing umbrella. Whether you're in a new or a mature market, spend time and energy on 'smart' pricing. Companies that deploy these effectively can drive significantly more revenue out of their product or service. There are great examples in the business world today. EasyJet have become experts in yield management, TDC in household telecom price management, Apple in global price control and strategies, and Google in pricing ads for specific search words.

When I joined EE, we would have been laughed out of town if we'd tried to class ourselves as experts in this area. But over time, the emergence and development of smart product management leaders who had a passion for pricing started to drive it forward. Not every product manager loves the complex and detailed minutiae of pricing. You need to find a few who want to do so before developing a new marketing idea.

Revenue of existing products and services is great, and needs to be managed and nurtured, but new revenue streams also require your attention. They are always small in the beginning and therefore do not get the necessary focus and resources. As a leader, you simply need to place a bet. I placed many bets with EE – 4G services, EETV, new Wi-Fi products, mobile advertising and chargeable after-sale services. Not all those new categories delivered, but some did and would not have done so unless they received an unfair (in relation to the size of the business) allocation of resources and attention.

Making sure that working capital works

A lot of leaders focus on P&L cash generation through revenue and cost management, but do not spend enough time driving working capital improvements. It is absolutely essential to secure a healthy working capital model by driving days of inventory *down,* driving payment terms of your suppliers *out,* and driving payment terms of your creditors *in.* My CFO used his purchasing teams to establish better payment terms with suppliers. This becomes easier if you consolidate your supplier base and can offer more volume per supplier in return for better payment terms. If you do not have enough leverage, you can at times buy yourself a solid working capital model by working with a bank. However, this is generally not cheap. Inventory management can only improve if you secure an aligned and integrated process between Marketing, Sales and Supply Chain. If you let any of these groups buy and manage inventory in isolation, you will be in bad shape. Marketing and Sales will make sure that you have enough stock for every customer to buy 20 different variations of the same product, and Supply Chain will make sure that your DIO – Days Inventory Outstanding[24] – is so good that Sales will have nothing to sell at the end of the quarter.

Finally, when you have optimized cost, revenue, and working capital (and you produce a lot of cash), it is important that you have a very clear and approved plan on what to do with it. If you do not have a plan, your shareholders will kindly ask you to send it back to them so that they can use it elsewhere, especially if your return on their capital employed is low.

As a leader, it is important that you understand how cash is generated – and lost – across your company. Equally, understand, monitor, and improve the balance sheet of your organization. Many leaders have been caught out because their balance sheet was over-leveraged. Companies that have too-high mortgages may falter even when their profit generation is healthy. On the flip side, if you do not have enough leverage, you may miss building out existing or new business opportunities. At EE, we always operated at below two times EBITDA, which is solid for a telecoms operator that generates a lot of cash.

The financial transformation of any company is the ultimate measurement of success or failure, but it is mostly the result of a successful business transformation.

The culmination of the joint venture

The final chapter in this book looks at what lies ahead for EE and the superfast boom it ignited.

We'll look at why BT purchased EE, what it means for their future and how the lessons we learned in integrating the Orange and T-Mobile businesses can be used to make future integrations even smoother.

With EE now embarking on another transformation, the opportunities for it to lead the future of mobility are greater than ever before. We'll look at how we got to this point, and how putting our people front and centre of the business drove our success.

A new transformation

In the late 1990s, just before the turn of the millennium, the Orange team grew out of their Bristol base and added a new office in London – 50 George Street in the heart of Marylebone. At that time, the Orange team were neighbours with Madonna and Guy Ritchie, Oasis's Noel Gallagher and various supermodels. It was the height of Cool Britannia and Orange, along with only a small band of other brands, led the way as one of Britain's brightest new businesses.

The Orange HQ entrance was a grand and imposing short tunnel, flanked with flaming torches on either side. A pair of automatic glass doors opened to visitors who would then be greeted by a marble staircase with the obligatory fish tank to the side (obligatory, because all of the Orange buildings – including the stores on the high street – were 'equipped' with a fish tank to meet the rigorous standards of the company's feng shui requirements).

On the third floor was the Imaginarium – the company's whacky but visionary strategy department – and the executive suites, including CEO Hans Snook's office.

From Snook's office, perfectly framed through a large window, one could see the BT Tower. Less than two miles from the Orange HQ, it was as if the team had purposely lined up the established British operator in its sights as their number one target – a daily reminder of the job in hand for a team who were looking to depose the fixed-line establishment with their talk of a future 'without wires'.

Over 15 years later, an evolved element of that same company finds itself a part of the very family it was once trying to unseat.

It's all change again in the British mobile sector. At the start of this book we looked at the ever-transforming nature of this industry. As I write this, BT's acquisition of EE has been approved and is starting to take shape, and the European authorities are reviewing a potential merger of Hutchison and Telefónica in the UK. This incestuous industry continues to consolidate. History repeats itself and a new era of communication competition emerges.

The BT and EE deal will be great for the UK. It will help make sure people the length and breadth of Britain are better connected wherever they are. In many countries across the world, customers can buy TV, fixed-line, Internet, and mobile services in a bundle, benefiting from better prices and additional services. The combination of BT and EE will be able to offer exactly this, bringing the UK market into line with the rest of the world.

The deal is also good for investment in Britain, not to mention jobs. It will encourage efficient investment in critical fixed and mobile infrastructure, helping make sure that the UK gets improvements in rural connectivity – as well as ultrafast broadband and 5G mobile – to stay ahead in the global economy. Both companies have demonstrated in the past that they are ready to invest to differentiate. Together, both companies have invested billions already.

The integration challenge

Having completed the transformation and sale of our business, I left EE in March 2016. My final day at the company was one of mixed emotions – sad to be leaving this great team, but proud of everything we had achieved together.

Now, a new team is responsible for the next tough challenge – another integration and another transformation as EE moves into the BT fold.

Historic merger and acquisition analysis – as well as my own experiences with EE – suggest that there are a number of critical success factors that underpin any successful corporate integration:

- The majority of management in each organization should focus on business-as-usual activities in order to minimize disruption to commercial momentum and to protect against disruptive activity by key competitors.

- Cross-company understanding and expertise should be leveraged jointly to develop clear transactional objectives that underpin and prioritize all integration activity.

- Suitable individuals should be hand-picked from both organizations to lead the integration activities and implement a robust governance process that doesn't limit speed of execution or adaptability.

- In order to manage the transition, the management of the acquirer needs to be respectful of the key leaders in the acquired entity regarding integration planning and decision making. Not doing so will disempower the existing management team, damage business-as-usual performance and destabilize key individuals across the business.

- Integration activity should always start as soon as possible (leveraging a clean team as required) to maximize the time available, respond to competitor activity and develop a robust day one action plan that can be implemented as soon as the transaction is complete.

- An organizational and management team structure should be designed to support the transaction rationale and corporate vision. It is critical to retain the core capabilities of the company that has been bought, and to retain exceptional agility and execution focus.
- Policies should be implemented to attract and retain employees who are fundamental to the delivery of the transaction rationale.
- A compelling communications strategy should be developed to keep employees of both organizations informed and engaged in the process.
- The development and execution of the consumer benefits should be prepared and articulated on day one of trading as the combined entity.
- The newly combined entity should maintain a relentless focus on customer experience across both business-as-usual and integration activities.[25] Key initiatives in this area should include:

  1 Putting customer retention in the transaction objectives and setting ambitious goals for this area.

  2 Embedding consideration of the customer experience as an integral part of merger planning.

  3 Identifying and accelerating actions to improve the customer experience across the combined entity.

  4 Communicating with and listening to customers (leveraging social media as required).

  5 Empowering employees by providing them with the tools and information they need to respond to customers caught up in the change.

The challenge for BT and EE in integrating their businesses is a huge one. But they have many experienced old hands who have seen transformation many times before and are no doubt putting the lessons of the past to good use.

Now, as an outsider looking in, I can't wait to see how it evolves. Watch this space.

5G and the video revolution

While BT's acquisition of EE is a major move forward for the UK's digital infrastructure, the future of the telecommunications market will not be shaped by the regulator or by big business events in the UK. Instead, global consumer demand will drive its evolution.

Businesses will lead the way in the investment of what is possible, but consumer appetite and adoption will be the ultimate accelerant.

Communications between human beings have become increasingly richer and more fun over time. During Microsoft's 'Windows at your fingertips' era in the 1980s, we were mostly engaging in e-mail and text-based communications. A few years on, and the digitization of photography and music enabled people to create more interesting personal content. Your music and your photos suddenly made every digital conversation more interesting. Today, iPads, larger-screen smartphones, 4G networks, and lower data pricing allow the inclusion of moving images with the integration of video and TV applications.

And that's where the next phase in telecommunications is heading. The next big leap will be with 5G. It's all about the moving image – video, TV, 3D and virtual reality – which will open a whole new world of communications, allowing you to combine real time with offline information in any format. You will be able to relive your vacation with your family, but explore that beach you didn't have time to visit. You can share and explore new digital experiences across video, text, photography, sounds, and touch. You will be able to live-broadcast yourself to your friends and family from everywhere. Many of these innovations are happening right now.

The richer data experience combined with an ever-increasing number of connected tools (smartphones, smartwatches, connected cameras, and tablets) along with the rise of the Internet of Things (where thousands of objects around you will be connected – from your clothing to your kitchen appliances, your car to the lamp posts on your street) will change people's work and private lives again.

The pure response time of 5G is astonishing. Its reaction time is predicted to be around one millisecond, unperceivable to a human, and about 50 times faster than 4G. Consequently, the potential benefits are amazing. It will be able to simplify complex environments, such as a port or manufacturing facility where there are thousands of moving parts, or a city centre, where traffic, people, stores, signage, and even parking meters interact, by connecting everything together through a single high-speed 5G network.

We will see a whole new world of applications and services emerge around 5G. It will enable cars to drive without accidents, utility companies to optimize energy and water supply, and real-time video companies to provide supervision for insurance and the emergency services. It also has the potential, through high-quality continuous video conferencing, to support even more flexible work environments. Imagine being 'transported' from your home to your office at the touch of a button. That's the future of 21st-century video conferencing once the networks can handle the required speeds.

4G was just the beginning. With next-generation technologies, there are thousands of new applications coming that will develop businesses and enrich people's lives.

The people of EE

Since the very first day of the formation of the joint venture in 2009, speculation had been rife about what France Telecom and Deutsche Telekom's long-term ambitions were for their merger of equals.

A flotation, a sale, a purchase, another merger? All of these options were put out there by industry watchers as potential end-game scenarios for the business that was created from Orange and T-Mobile.

The truth is that, throughout the five-year journey, there were many scenarios evaluated and many end-games investigated, but there was no one single overriding masterplan from day one. In business, there rarely is such certainty.

What was certain, however, was that the two businesses intended to create huge value from the formation of Britain's biggest mobile communications company, and deliver a step change in expectation and delivery for Britain's business and consumer customers.

It succeeded in both ambitions.

Over the three and- a half years in which we built, launched and transformed EE, one of the critical factors in our success was, of course, our people. As a business, you are nothing without your people – especially a business with such a significant front-line sales and service team as ours. Out of our 15,000 employees, around 10,000 held some sort of front-line role and were dealing with customers.

Both Orange and T-Mobile had found some success in driving loyalty and results from their employees – but it was far from optimum. From the moment the joint venture was announced in 2009, and during a seriously tough year of integration in 2010, employee engagement and motivation dropped like a stone. Uncertainty, fear and a lack of clarity in the purpose of the mission was having a significantly detrimental effect on how people felt – and how they delivered for the business.

Driving up the employee Net Promoter Score

In the summer of 2011, EE's employee Net Promoter Score (eNPS) was –12. High-performing organizations would look for an eNPS of +20 and higher. We were a long way from heaven. In fact, many of our employees were telling us that they were in employee hell. As a collective, the organization had managed to achieve its goal of keeping the business and its brands on track – but at a price. People were disillusioned, confused and frustrated. There were more Detractors than Promoters. Our employees were telling us that Everything Everywhere Ltd was a gloomy place.

During the transformation of the company, we were able to lift morale and passion in a number of clear ways:

1 Our big and bold vision, mission and purpose were credible and people believed in them.

2 We simplified the organization and gave people more responsibility for delivery. Importantly, we also implemented more accountability than before, meaning that there were rewards for success, and consequences for not getting results.

3 We made sure the leadership team was more visible than ever before – in all parts of the organization but especially on the front line.

4 We put a consistent drumbeat of communications in place to ensure people knew what was going on and what was expected of them.

5 We developed a rigour around the calendar of company activities – town hall meetings and WebEx's for our quarterly financial results, top 400 senior leadership meetings twice a year, plus a further two top 100 director events.

These were essential elements of driving employee engagement, and they created a level of mutual respect between the employee and the company. But above all of this, I believe the sense of being successful as a team – of 15,000 people – really pushed us forward.

We moved from an eNPS of –26 in September 2010 to an eNPS of +30 in November 2014, just a few weeks before it was announced that BT were in talks to buy the business.

Between those two dates, we were named as one of the top 25 big companies to work for by *The Sunday Times* employee satisfaction partner Best Companies. These results were remarkable and were a reason for – and a result of – our success in driving transformation within the company.

In a cold and wet country like the UK, an eNPS score of over 25 is solid. While working for France Telecom, I remember a visit to one of my Orange subsidiaries in the Caribbean. The operation was successful and the sun shone every day. Guess what – we had an eNPS of over 90! People were super motivated. During one employee session, where I asked what we needed to improve in Orange Dominican Republic, I was met with a stony silence. Most employees were not used to engaging with the CEO to talk about the company. Finally, someone broke the deadlock. An employee stood up and screamed, 'There are no issues here – we love Orange Dominican Republic.' Immediately afterwards, others stood up and did the same with tears in their eyes. They were clapping, crying, dancing. As a typical cynical European, I immediately thought that I was being tricked – this was surely all prepared. Employees in Europe – especially Northern Europe – discuss and critique their company. It is not in their make-up to show too much positive emotion towards their employer. Do that, and they will start thinking you're an oddball who is not objective and, most worryingly, does not require a salary increase! It is simply not done – there is always something to complain about. Well, that's not the case in the Dominican Republic, where the sun always shines and you've got a job. So, with different countries you need different eNPS targets.

Regardless, you won't be able to unleash the data that your eNPS score gives you unless you break it down across each functional organization, each office location, and each major topic.

At EE, we broke it down into seven areas – Personal Growth, Leadership, My Company, My Manager, Fair Deal, Working Together, and Wellbeing.

This helped us to understand where we were doing well and which areas needed development. The two problem areas we worked hard to improve were Personal Growth and Working Together. People told us that they didn't feel that they were able to develop within the organization and found it tough to work across functional organizations. As a leadership team, we put in significant amounts of work to resolve these issues.

On the flip side, Leadership, My Company and My Manager were really positive. People understood the vision, the plan, their role and what was expected of them.

The individual areas will tell you a story and give you a bearing on what to focus on next. However, it is essential that you read some of the specific written feedback from your people. Done in an anonymous way, this is like therapy for your employees! They will gladly offer up their darkest frustrations and it gives you further insight on what is really bothering them. As well as giving your employees a platform, often you'll find that the root causes of the problems they expose are ones that directly link to poor performance in an area of your business.

Quite simply, if you do not have motivated employees, you cannot achieve your goals. They are the fuel for your business transformation – it starts and ends with them.

Employee motivation is driven primarily by a clear understanding of the purpose of a company. If the purpose of the company is positive for society, then your people will understand why they come to work beyond paying off the mortgage. This is the key to employee motivation.

Ultimately, our employees became truly engaged because they were the architects of a unique story in business history. They were able to transform a number three and a number four in the market and create a true industry leader, delivering the best mobile network in Europe that will enable millions of people today and in years to come to keep close to the people, places and things they like, wherever they are, whenever they want. They were part of a movement that took the UK from last in line to front of the pack. They kick-started a revolution that gave Britain a digital infrastructure to rival the rest of the world.

Who were those people? *They* were EE.

Large-scale transformation of any major business is no easy task. It is a hugely complex web of interconnected issues, systems, functions, departments and people.

As a leader, you need to be the torch bearer for change and cut your way through the problems, setting out a clear vision and way forward for your business and your employees.

Integrating businesses is a tough job. At its heart is the cultural challenge, which can often be an emotionally charged affair. But the rational rules I've outlined in this final chapter – the lessons I learned as we brought together Orange and T-Mobile to become EE – will stand you in good stead.

The digital age is still in its infancy. Compared to the timeline of the industrial revolution, we are at the point where a few new steam-powered factories have started to pop up on the agricultural land of our forefathers. All around us, the land is still green – but it's about to undergo a dramatic change.

There is a tsunami of technological innovation that is heading our way over the coming decades. 5G will be the next key driver of a new world of disruption. Communities, cities, citizens and corporations will all feel the change.

So, the final question to ask yourself: is your business ready for the transformation?

AFTERWORD

So, that was the EE story. I hope you found it useful, insightful and, above all, practical, with lessons and learnings that you can apply to your own business – whatever stage of transformation it's in.

We've taken in a lot of subjects and themes in this book – from the importance of leadership style to the importance of rigid performance management practices. We've looked at how a brand is essential to a business, and how strategic partnerships can help you grow your company in ways that would be tougher if you were operating in isolation.

When we truly boil it down, I believe there are three key elements to delivering a successful transformation – starting with purpose.

Purpose

Ask yourself, 'What is the purpose of my business?' Your initial assessment will probably be 'to make money' or 'drive the value of the business'. This is true, and we shouldn't be embarrassed about that fact. We should celebrate it. The metrics and KPIs that go alongside those simple phrases, 'to make money' or 'to drive the value', are essential in driving a business toward success. But there is a need to create something more. Something beyond the cold hard metrics of the financial success story. I firmly believe that every business needs to identify its purpose beyond the balance sheet. At EE, that was about building the UK's best network and service – creating a digital legacy for the country that would benefit its citizens, its communities and its businesses. Whether that was through the ability to do business wherever, whenever and however they wanted, or simply giving them the opportunity to watch a funny cat video on YouTube while on the bus – it didn't matter. The central essence of what we were doing at EE was positive change. Because of what we did, people would be able to do something that they couldn't do before. This was not just about positive change within our business, but about positive change in terms of the impact we would have outside of our business. We wrapped it up in the brand mantra, 'Now You Can'. It drove our thinking, our development cycles and our way of doing business. It was about doing something good for society – not just your shareholders. And not doing good because you need to be seen to do the right thing, but because it *is* the right thing. It's easy for this idea of 'the do-good business' to get lost in corporate responsibility initiatives or fluffy plans that make people feel good but have no link back to your business. Don't get lost down this road. It does no good for your employees, your business, your customers, or society. Find your business's true purpose beyond the balance sheet. Ensure it links back to the fundamentals of what your business does. The resulting effect is likely to be a win–win for all involved, and will ultimately drive consideration, loyalty and trust from consumers.

Process

In Chapter 5, we looked at the importance of the Performance Management Framework. This was the backbone of the success of EE. It can be considered a dry subject, but it is of huge importance. After all, if you're not measuring the right things, then you're not going to be able to drive the business in the right way. You're not going to be able to tell what's going right (and do more of it) or wrong (and how to change it). The processes in your business will make or break your success. If they are too draconian and bureaucratic, they will slow you down, cause frustration, disenfranchise your people and lead them to focus on administrative tasks, rather than killing the competition. Too loose and free, and you will encourage chaos and risk, leaving you vulnerable to random decision making at the whim of individuals, and a lack of focus. The challenge is to find the sweet spot – the process nirvana where you have a way of doing business that drives control and enables measurement, but also encourages entrepreneurial thinking and accountability at all levels. The bigger your business, the harder it is to do this. Different-sized businesses need different levels of process. A start-up of three people around a kitchen table will be an easier beast to tame than an established corporation. Supertankers are tougher to turn than speedboats, which is why process and rigour are so important in a supertanker's transformation. Without them, you simply can't turn the wheel. So first, ask yourself – what size of business am I trying to transform and how much process do we need to ensure we drive rigour and measurement, without losing creativity and free thinking?

People

If Purpose was the heart and Process was the backbone, then the People of EE were its soul. Having the right people in the right place doing the right things is an absolute essential in driving every business success. Big or small, start-up or established – it doesn't matter. Your people are your business. Along with the factories, the infrastructure and the product itself, your people are a strategic asset of your business. At EE, I took some tough decisions early on to ensure that we were a nimble and dynamic organization that could deliver on the business performance and purpose. That meant losing some good people straight off the bat. But it also meant empowering my new team to deliver in a way that would have been impossible in an otherwise fat and slow organization. We put in place the support of the right teams, the right structures and the right interdependencies – with clear roles and responsibilities – to ensure our business became a well-oiled machine that worked as one.

If you're leading a business transformation, I wish you every success. Transforming a business is never easy. It's a risky business and most fail or, rather, never truly reach their potential. EE was one of the exceptions. By focusing on the fundamentals outlined in this book, we changed the way we ran the business, what it stood for, how it looked, and what it delivered – for its shareholders, for its employees, and for its customers.

ENDNOTES

1 I must say, I find it wonderfully gratifying that I'm able to discover more about the creation of the web through the web itself, and freely admit that I gleaned this information from Wikipedia.

2 Yuval Noah Harari (2015) *Sapiens: A Brief History of Humankind*, Vintage, London.

3 Definition of Moore's Law taken from http://www.mooreslaw.org.

4 Source: Gartner.

5 Joseph Waring (2014) Number of devices to hit 4.3 per person by 2020 – report, *Mobile World Live*, 16 October [online] http://www. mobileworldlive.com/featured-content/home-banner/ connected-devices-to-hit-4-3-per-person-by-2020-report/.

6 30th anniversary of the Vodafone name, *Vodafone* [online] http:// www.vodafone.com/content/index/media/vodafone-group-releases/2014/30th-anniversary.html.

7 Number of mobile (cellular) subscriptions worldwide from 1993 to 2015 (in millions) [online] http://www.statista.com/statistics/262950/ global-mobile-subscriptions-since-1993/.

8 The first commercial mobile phone with a built-in camera was manufactured by Samsung and released in South Korea at the turn of the new millennium. They built the world's first commercially available watchphone too.

9 The first commercial mobile phones cost around $4,000 when launched in 1983. Today, you can walk out of a store with a subsidized phone and a monthly contract having paid nothing up front.

10 EBITDA is a financial indicator that stands for Earnings before Interest, Taxes, Depreciation and Amortization.

11 Source: Orange GFK data c.2010 (internal report).

12 In October 2011, Australia's Reibey Institute found that over three- and five-year periods, ASX500 companies with women directors delivered significantly higher return on equity (ROE) than those companies without any women on their boards. There are countless other studies that reveal the same results. The last time I checked, the world population has approximately the same number of men and women. Women are also higher performers in school and university compared to their male colleagues.

13 'Bumping' is when managers who fall out of a top layer are pushed down into the next one. This results in a situation where your expensive managers do not lose their jobs but are demoted while retaining their existing salary. You must avoid this.

14 Walter Isaacson (2011) *Steve Jobs: The Exclusive Biography*, Simon & Schuster, New York.

15 At 38 hours per person per month (Source: EE Internal analysis 2011/12).

16 In fact, according to the CBI, the number of UK mobile subscriptions would surpass many other nations in 2013. They were right. They did.

17 Revealed as an average of 77 minutes per day by the *Guardian* newspaper in 2012.

18 Michael Mankins and Richard Steele (2011) Turning great strategy into great performance, *Harvard Business Review*, July.

19 'Orange Wednesdays' was a 2-for-1 cinema ticket deal that allowed Orange customers to get an extra cinema ticket for a friend on a Wednesday. It ran for 10 years and was one of the most successful loyalty campaigns the marketing industry has ever seen. It was a huge retention driver for Orange.

20 The Hollywood actor Kevin Bacon would become the celebrity figurehead in our TV ads from day one, teaching the UK public about the magic of 4G. He was a great sport and did a great job for us.

21 All information taken from the EE Mobile Living Index, which was published in August 2013. The results were brought together using insight from the EE network team and an independent TNS survey of 1,000 4G users. The information itself was gathered between 1 January 2013 and 31 July 2013. TNS conducted the survey of 4GEE customers in May, using telephone research. https://explore-orange-live-orangedigital.s3.amazonaws.com/2013/08/19/4GEEMobileLiving IndexFINALFINAL.pdf

22 Source: The EE Brand Health Check, May 2013 (internal report).

23 Source: Q4 2012 EE Consumer Mobile Review (internal report).

24 DIO stands for Days Inventory Outstanding. It refers to the number of days your inventory sits in your stores and your warehouse before it is sold to the end customer. The lower the number the better, unless it constrains customer demand. You can manage this number down with improved forecasting, shorter delivery and supply chain processes, but also by negotiating shorter inventory ownership with suppliers. Here, for example, your supplier will still own the stock, even when it stands in your warehouse or your store.

25 Academic studies have found that more than half of all mergers fail to deliver the intended improvement in shareholder value, with customer defections a key contributor to the high failure rate.

INDEX

afterword (on) 183–85
 people 185
 process 184–85
 purpose 183–84
Alexander, T 16, 19, 30, 50
Allera, M 112, 113–14
announcing EE (and) 101–21
 the communications challenge
  (and) 110–17
  'breaking cover' – the
   reveal 111–16
  launch success through employee
   engagement 116–17
  launch timetable 111
 importance of strategic
  partnerships 107–10
  driving competitive
   differentiation
   through 108–10
 launch project
  management 103–05
 managing the pressure
  points 101–07
  but 'no plan B' 105–07
 new website goes live 115
 'Project 11' 103
 project management and
  partnerships 120–21
 'we are EE' 118–21
an audacious plan 49–62
 big bang theory 49–51
  key elements for 50
 building a plan and vision
  for the company
  (and/by) 58–62
  authenticity as key 61–62
  establishing power of
   purpose 59
  vision 58–59
 innovation vs regulation
  conundrum 51–58
  launching 4G without required
   spectrum 53

 legalities of 54–55
 mobile spectrum – fourth
  generation (4G) 51–52
 working with governments and
  regulators 55–58
Apple 60, 81, 91, 94, 104, 108
 iMac 12
 iPhone / iPhone 4G version 12, 117
article on why businesses fail (*Harvard
 Business Review*, 2011) 64

Bacon, K 116
Berners-Lee, T 2, 11
brand transformation (and) 77–87
 core of a new brand 80–82
 creation of a new brand 83–85
 estimating costs for 82
 maintenance of existing
  brands 86–87
 new brand guidelines 85–86
 rationale for a new brand 79–80
brands 75–80 *see also* building a new
  brand for Britain
 DNA of 79
British Telecom (BT) 108
 Cellnet 9, 10, 13, 16
 purchase of EE 173–77 *see also*
  culmination of joint venture
building a new brand for Britain
 (through) 75–100
 brand transformation 77–87
 a brand-new DNA (and) 96–100
  company (DNA) values 98–100
   see also values (EE)
  culture 97–98
  teamwork 96–97
 product innovation (and) 87–96
  big business 95–96
  going back to the core 89–92
  list of problems in launching 4G
   92–93
  tackling big hurdles 93–95
 the secret project 75–77

Cameron, D 134
CAPEX 89–90, 93
challenge of momentum (and) 123–46
    ever-evolving network/superfast
        connectivity 133–36
    serving half of Britain (and) 136–46
        creating customer loyalty/the NPS
            tool set 142–45
        fixing the service basics 137
        a tough ambition see customer
            service
    technological transformation
        126–33 see also IT lessons
    2013–2014: the superfast
        years 123–26
        driving change in customer
            behaviour 124–26
connectivity 2, 6, 7, 119,
        134, 174
    and customer loyalty 142
    importance of 8
    in society 9–12
Cook, T (CEO, Apple) 94
culmination of the joint venture
        (and) 173–82
    5G and the video revolution 177–78
    the integration challenge 175–76
        critical success factors
            for 175–76
    a new transformation: BT and EE
        deal
        173–74
    the people of EE (and) 178–82
        driving employee
            engagement 179–80
        employee Net PromoterScore
            (eNPS) 179–81
        motivation 181–82
customer service (and) 138–41
    aiming to be number one
        in 138–39
    basics for 139–41
    Propensity to Call (PTC) reduction
        programme 138–39

digital PR 116
Dominican Republic 180–81

EBITDA 18, 81, 165, 169, 171, 186
European Competition Commission
        22–23, 26

Everything Everywhere (EE) 83
    Business Transformation Programme
        (BTP) 167–68
    Clone Phone 119
    film store and new services 119
    in-house outsourced centre
        (Moldova) 168
    purchased by BT 25

Facebook 10, 34, 78, 81, 88, 116
figure: EE Performance Management
        Framework 67
the five Es – experience, education,
        energy, empathy and
        ethics 39–40
5G 177–78
Ford, H 29, 91
4G 52
    Apple iPhone 117
    breaking records 147–48
    customer behaviour 124–26
    device range at launch 115
    4GEE 116–17
    inaugural cities 120
    network services in
        Scandinavia 90, 91
    problems in launching 92–93
France Telecom (FT) 19,
        168–69, 180
    and Deutsche Telekom merger 178

Gates, B 13
General Motors (GM) 33, 72
Germany (and)
    Deutsche Post 81
    Deutsche Telekom (DT) 19, 94, 169,
        178
Gerstner, L (IBM) 101
Google 6, 10, 84, 88, 108, 170

Harvard Business Review 64, 148
Huawei 108
Hurd, M 13, 128, 148
Hutchison Telecom Orange and
        Mercury One2One 10

IBM 33, 34, 138, 159, 168
inspiration, inventors and
        innovation 1–13 see also
        subject entries
    transformative leaders 2–5

transformative technologies 5–8
    connectivity 8
    rise of technology 6–7
transformative telecoms
        market 8–13 *see also subject entry*
IT lessons (and) 127–33
    environment categories 131–33
        change management 131
        disaster recovery and replication systems/processes 132
        incident management process 131
        new application development and delivery 132–33
        pro-active health management systems/processes 131–32
    Randy Mott quotes 128–29 *see also* Mott, R
    simple ratios for guidance 129–30
        cost 129–30
        reliability 130
        time to market of new functionality 130

Japan (and) 52
    4G network 91
    NTT Docomo 90
Jobs, S 49, 60
Johnson, B 115
the joint venture 15–27
    Britain's biggest communication company (and) 22–27
        'business as usual' 24–6
        creation of Everything Everywhere 26–27
        EC approval 26
        integration planning and 'clean room' groups 23–24
        learnings from the merger 25
    critical success factors for 21–22 *see also* success factors
    genesis of 16–22
        the big deal 18–19
        dealing with the brands 19–20
        finalizing the deal: French and German teams 17–18

key performance indicators (KPIs) 66, 70, 71–72, 183

leaders *see also* transformative leaders
    the traditional product business leader 155
    the web entrepreneur 155
    the web marketer 155
    the web techie 155
leadership by example 73
leadership structure (and) 29–37
    evolving the business 30–31
    mapping out the structure (by/ with) 32–37
        functions 34–35
        measurement 36–37
        priorities 33–34
        profit and loss (P&L) models 32–33
        simplicity 32–33
        size 35
        symbolism 35–36
        time 32
    organizational design principles 31
leadership styles 44–47
    credibility and authenticity in 46
    differences in 45
    key attributes for 46
    to match business challenge 47

Mercury One2One 10, 11, 13
Microsoft 34, 91, 108, 177
Moat, R 16, 19, 30, 50
mobility 8, 173
    as fundamental 82
Moore's law 6
Mott, R 127–29
    quotes from 128–29
Musion 3D 'hologram' technology 118

Net Promoter Score (NPS) 137, 142, 144–45
the new team (and) 29–47
    establishing priorities and SWOT 43
    leadership structure to enable transformation 29–37 *see also* leadership structure
    new leadership style for a new business 44–47 *see also* leadership styles
    selecting people 37–40
        and diversity/gender diversity 38
        and the five E concepts 39–40

the new team (and) (*cont.*)
    interested in working as a
      team 38–39
    in line with company values 39
    with potential and attitude to
      change 38
    from within the business 39
  transforming the management
    structure 40–43
    to avoid miscommunication 40
    EE principles for 41–42
    by spans and layers
      discipline 41–43
Nokia 7, 91, 107
Now You Can 83, 84

Orange 7, 11, 12, 16, 17, 18, 19, 20,
    22–24, 26–27, 30, 50, 52, 76,
    78, 79, 80, 84, 86–87, 93, 97,
    102, 103, 104, 112, 115, 120,
    136, 148, 150, 162, 173–74,
    178–79
  Dominican Republic 180–81
  and France Telecom 16
  Rabbit service 10
O'Reilly, C 75
O2 30, 52, 126

pay as you go mobile services 76, 78, 126
Performance Management Framework
    66, 67
Philippines 52, 140
profit and loss (P&L) structures 32–33

Samsung 91, 94, 108
sleeping with the enemy *see* the joint
    venture
sleeplessness 109–10
Sloan, A P 72 (General Motors) 72
Snook, H (CEO Orange) 10–11, 174
Sony 109
Sorrell, Sir M 165
South Korea 52, 60, 90, 91, 94, 134, 186
step change in performance (and/and
    the) 63–74
  aligning performance to the
    vision 67–68
  execution 63–65
  frontline teams/knowing the
    customer 72–74

  instilling clear accountabilities and
    responsibilities 69–70
  Performance Dashboard 71–72
  Performance Management
    Framework 66, 67, 74
  setting the direction and defining
    priorities 68–69
  team commitment 70–71
    structure for memos on 70
success factors: ambition,
    empowerment, transparency,
    governance, decisions, adopt
    and go 21–22
Sunday Times, The 84
  100 Best Companies to Work
    For (2015) 25
  Best Companies 180
supercharging sales (and/by) 147–63
  breaking records with 4G 147–49
  digital transformation 154–58 *see
    also* leaders
  and the multi-channel
    future 157–58
  points to consider for 156–57
  retail transformation (and/
    through) 150–54
  principles for building reward
    incentives 153
  retail equals detail 153–54
  the right shops and right
    people 151–52
  the science sales
    compensation 152–53
  transforming a business-to-
    business function (and)
    149, 158–63
  account satisfaction process 162
  annual account coverage review
    process 161–62
  B2B sales force
    assessment 159–60
  executive sponsorship and
    lighthouse account
    process 162
  five-step sales process 160–61
  major account planning
    process 161
  transforming a business-to-
    consumer function 149–50
SWOT analysis 43

Three 13, 126
3G 52, 125, 134
T-Mobile 17, 18, 19, 20, 22–24,
    26–27, 30, 50, 52, 76, 78, 80,
    84, 86–87, 93, 97, 102, 103,
    104, 112, 116, 120, 136, 148,
    150, 162, 178–79
transformative leaders 2–5
  Berners-Lee, Sir T 2
  Gates, B 3–4, 5
  Hurd, M 5
transformative telecoms market
    (and) 8–13
  connectivity in society 9–12
  impact of technological change 13
  mergers, sales and
    rebrandings 12–13
  'smart' phones 12–13
tweeter, the rogue 113–14
the £12.5 billion business
    (and) 165–71
  driving revenue profitability
    (by) 169–71
    ensuring that working capital
      works 170–71
    smart pricing management 170
  the importance of cash
    management 167–68
  the key to supplier
    management 168–69

kick-starting a financial
    transformation
    165–67
Twitter 116–17
2G renewal programme 93

United Kingdom (UK)
  Government: bidding for new 4G
    spectrum 52
  Office of Fair Trading 22
United States (US) (and) 52, 60, 91
  4G network 91
  Verizon 90

values of EE 99–100
  be bold 99
  be brilliant 99–100
  be clear 99
Virgin 84, 126
  Mobile 17
Vodafone 10, 17, 30, 52, 78, 84, 126,
    150, 162
  merges with Mannesmann 12
  Racal 9

Which? 136–37

YouTube 11, 78

Zuckerberg, M 11